INDIA
INSIDE

Also by the Authors

Nirmalya Kumar, *Marketing as Strategy:*
Understanding the CEO's Agenda for Driving
Growth and Innovation
(Boston: Harvard Business School Press, 2004)

Nirmalya Kumar, *Global Marketing*
(India: Business World, 2006)

Nirmalya Kumar and Jan-Benedict E. M.
Steenkamp, *Private Label Strategy:*
How to Meet the Store Brand Challenge
(Boston: Harvard Business School Press, 2007)

James C. Anderson, Nirmalya Kumar,
and James A. Narus, *Value Merchants:*
Demonstrating and Documenting Superior
Value in Business Markets (Boston: Harvard
Business School Press, 2007)

Nirmalya Kumar with Pradipta K. Mohapatra
and Suj Chandrasekhar, *India's Global*
Powerhouses: How They Are Taking on the World
(Boston: Harvard Business Press, 2009)

NIRMALYA KUMAR / PHANISH PURANAM

INDIA INSIDE

THE EMERGING INNOVATION CHALLENGE TO THE WEST

HARVARD BUSINESS REVIEW PRESS

BOSTON, MASSACHUSETTS

Library of Congress Cataloging-in-Publication Data

Kumar, Nirmalya.
  India inside : the emerging innovation challenge to the West / Nirmalya Kumar, Phanish Puranam.
    p. cm.
  ISBN 978-1-4221-5875-3 (alk. paper)
  1. Technological innovations—India.   2. Diffusion of innovations—India.   3. New products—India.   4. Research, Industrial—India.
I. Puranam, Phanish.   II. Title.
  HC440.T4K86 2012
  338'.0640954—dc23

                                                    2011021193

To Surabhi, my sister

Innovation's mirror is constancy;

thank you for always being there

—NK

To Panchali, my wife

For making this possible

—PP

Contents

Preface

When we were children growing up in India, it was drilled into us, both at school and at home, what an old and great civilization India was. We were taught about the discoveries and inventions that India had offered to the world over the centuries.

Our history lessons began with the Indus Valley civilization, which flourished between 3300 and 1300 BC. This always led to a fascinating discussion of the urban planning system at Mohenjo-Daro (now in Pakistan), one of the largest cities of the civilization, excavated in the 1930s. The city is believed to have had the world's first urban sanitation system. Individual homes obtained water from municipal wells and had a room that was apparently set aside for bathing, from which wastewater was directed to covered drains that lined the major streets.

Our mathematics teachers invariably mentioned that India gave the world the concept of zero and the decimal system. While today we are aware that these observations are subject to considerable debate, we took them at face value as schoolchildren. For us, it was a demonstration of India's long history of contributions to the world of science and mathematics. Famous Indian mathematicians, astronomers, and other scientists—from Aryabhata in the fifth to sixth century, to Bhaskara I and Bhramagupta in the seventh century, all the way to Ramanujam and Bose in the early twentieth century— were superstars for us.

How could we not aspire to go to university, having been taught that Nalanda, in northeastern India, was one of the earliest full-fledged universities in the world? It had been functioning as a center of learning from 497 AD on. Nalanda, meaning "insatiable in giving," was devoted to Buddhist studies, but it also imparted education in the arts, astronomy, mathematics, medicine, and politics. At its peak, its dormitories and libraries had two thousand professors educating ten thousand students, supposedly attracted from as far away as China, Greece, Japan, Persia, and Turkey. Nalanda died a slow death between the eleventh and twelfth centuries, around the time when the oldest surviving Western universities, Bologna in Italy and Oxford in England, began their life.

Having grown up with these beliefs as schoolchildren, we arrived at university and the first serious consideration of career opportunities, and had to confront the painful realities of contemporary India. Ironically, the Indus Valley irrigation system was better than that which existed in parts of modern India! Most of the recent "Indian" advances in science were made by those of our compatriots who had migrated to the West and pursued their discoveries at famous American and European universities. Our families include scholars with international reputations, but watching their efforts to produce world-class research within the constraints of Indian universities helped make salient the disparity of working conditions between what they faced and what their Western collaborators faced.

Instead, we observed that innovation in India had contorted itself mainly into an ingenuity to overcome import, licensing, and other bureaucratic controls. The most popular concepts in industrial innovation were the CKD (completely knocked down) units that were imported and subsequently assembled in India using "screwdriver technology" and "reverse engineering" (no explanation is necessary). Given this reality, as was the case for the majority of the graduating classes of elite Indian educational institutions, we headed to the United States for postgraduate studies. Yet, while Indian innovation seemed to have gone into hiding, Indian entrepreneurship in the broadest sense of the word never did. It was alive and well in the form of *jugaad*, or the concept of making the best of a situation and inventing solutions to problems using limited resources, through a combination of imagination, creativity, and even cunning.

It took a decade after the initiation of the economic liberalization in 1991 to get the country's business houses and economy in order. The pulls of family and, to our pleasant surprise, work saw us returning to India with increasing frequency. We could not help but notice a country that appeared to be taking the first steps toward becoming a serious player in the innovation space. This book was prompted by the question as to whether these steps could lead to a giant leap for Indian innovation, with the "Made in India" label becoming synonymous with innovation. Our research led us to realize that perhaps this is not the correct frame of reference. Instead, as we contend in this book, "India Inside" can be just as synonymous with innovation as "Made in India." Through several recommendations we make at the end of each chapter, we hope to provide some answers for both policy makers and companies in India and the West. But because Indian innovation is still an emerging story, there is ample opportunity for countries and firms to shape the trajectory of this phenomenon. As a result, we also hope that the book will raise many questions about the future of Indian innovation and its implications for the West.

This book builds on the previous work of pioneering colleagues such as C. K. Prahalad's bottom of the pyramid and Vijay Govindarajan's reverse-innovation concepts. Our goal, however, is not to restrict Indian innovation to what is visible to end users in the developed world. Instead, we propose that Indian innovation can be a ubiquitous, invisible force originating out of India.

Some of our colleagues have asked us why we did not write a comparative assessment of India *and* China. While some of the analysis in this book does compare India and China, the focus of this book is unambiguously on India. This is not to deny that China will very likely be as important as India, if not more important than India, on the global innovation stage in the coming years. Yet, India and China are large enough, important enough, and interesting enough in their own right to merit dedicated books on each single country alone. Moreover, we as authors simply do not know China the way we know India. Consider this, then, if you will, a book by people who know and care about India.

Acknowledgments

Our first and deepest gratitude is to all the managers, academics, and policy makers who took time from their busy schedules to meet with us. Therefore, we start by thanking those who met with us to share their insights:

V. Bharathwaj, 24/7 Customer

T. Hariharan, 24/7 Customer

Mohit Jain, 24/7 Customer

P. V. Kannan, 24/7 Customer

Kumar Mangalam Birla, Aditya Birla Group

Subhash Bana, Alcatel-Lucent

Pratap Reddy, Apollo Hospitals

Anandh Balasundaram, AstraZeneca

Tanjore Balganesh, AstraZeneca

Sudhir Nambiar, AstraZeneca

Baba N. Kalyani, Bharat Forge

Vinita Bali, Britannia

Pradipta K. Mohapatra, Business Coaching Foundation
    India

Samir K. Brahmachari, CSIR and DSIR

Naresh Kumar, CSIR

Acknowledgments

Satish Reddy, Dr. Reddy's Laboratories

Sudeep Kumar, CSIR

V. K. Gupta, CSIR

Sarv Saravanan, EMC

Aniruddho Basu, Ericsson

Ashish Gupta, Evaluserve

Marc Vollenweider, Evaluserve

Siddharth Nambiar, Evaluserve

Guillermo Wille, General Electric

Mano Manoharan, General Electric

Gopichand Katragadda, General Electric

Ashok Kumar, Government of India

Kanwaljit Singh, Helion

Rishi Krishnan, IIM Bangalore

S. K. Nandy, Indian Institute of Science

V. Rajaraman, Indian Institute of Science

Subhash Dhar, Infosys

Sanjay Mohan, Infosys

Sanjay Purohit, Infosys

Akash Deep Batra, Infosys

Rahul Bedi, Intel

Kishore Ramisetty, Intel

Praveen Vishakantaiah, Intel

Rahul Agarwal, Erehwon Consulting

Kumar Parakala, KPMG

Harsh Mariwala, Marico

Srini Koppolu, Microsoft

Nina Choudhuri, Microsoft

Ajay Piramal, Piramal Enterprises

Somesh Sharma, Piramal Enterprises

Bomi Gagrat, Pfizer Ltd.

Sunil Madhok, Pfizer Ltd.

Wido Menhardt, Philips

Vandana Subramanian, Philips

Erik M. Vermeulen, Philips

S. Bhaskaran, Philips

Harsh Dhand, Philips

Sudarshan K. Arora, Ranbaxy

Sandeep Singhal, Sequoia Capital India Advisors

Siddharth A. Pai, TPI Advisory Services India

I. Vijaya Kumar, Wipro Technologies

V. R. Venkatesh, Wipro Technologies

We were fortunate to be supported by a great team during the course of our research. A special thanks to Tufool Al-Nuaimi, Karin Baye, Suruchi Bhargava, Donna Everett, Eddie Guzdar, and Suseela Yesudian.

Prashant Bhardwaj helped us gain access to his network of managers and academics in Bengaluru. Aniruddho Basu deserves special thanks for carefully reading and sharing comments on early drafts. We also thank our coauthors, Kannan Srikanth (ISB), Saikat Chaudhuri (Wharton), Suma Athreye (Brunel), Tufool Al-Nuaimi and Gerry George (Imperial), on various research projects about innovation in India, insights of which infuse this book.

The research costs for this book were partly borne by the Management Innovation Lab (led by Professor Julian Birkinshaw) and the Centre for Marketing at London Business School. Our own research has been continuously supported by the Aditya Birla India Centre at London Business School. The school and we are grateful to Kumar Mangalam Birla for generously funding the Centre in his father's memory.

1

Where Are the Indian Googles, iPods, and Viagras?

OVER TWO DECADES, India has established itself as the global hub for software development and back-office services. The story of how Indian software engineers capitalized on the millennium-bug scare to create an information technology (IT) services juggernaut has inspired countless other Indian firms to attempt to repeat the same feat for customer contact, analytics, legal, and medical transcription services. In many of these segments, India has achieved a dominant share of the offshore market, with estimates that India accounts for 65 percent of the global offshore IT industry and 45 percent of the global business process outsourcing industry.[1]

Moving work offshore to India has had some inescapable implications for the mobility of white-collar jobs in the Western world. The traditional concern in the West has been about immigrants coming onshore to compete for local jobs; now, the effects of that competition can be felt from distant offshore locations such as India. Although estimates of the extent of the flight of jobs from the developed world to India remain embroiled in controversy, there is little doubt that the process has caused considerable angst in the West. Support for free trade has fallen as people in the developed world have grown alarmed by its perceived threats, rather than charmed by its potential virtues. Thus, in a recent global poll of forty-seven countries, the United States came in dead last in the percentage of the population supporting free trade.[2]

Yet many Western elites argue that this fear is misplaced, because the distinctive advantage, still monopolized by the developed world, is innovation. For example, in *The World Is Flat*, Thomas Friedman argues that apprehension about free trade is based on the mistaken assumption "that everything that is going to be invented has been invented, and that therefore economic competition is a zero-sum game."[3] In his view, innovation and idea generation will continue to keep Western companies and populations economically supreme, with the "more sophisticated tasks being done in the developed world and the less sophisticated tasks in the developing world—where each has its comparative advantage."[4] The more aggressive proponents in this camp offer a powerful retort to the conjecture that India can make the transition from services to innovation: "So where are the Indian Googles, iPods, and Viagras?"

The conventional wisdom in India seems to echo this view.[5] While recognizing their own achievements, many Indian managers we met in the course of our research for this book repeatedly expressed their opinion that providing services on demand was one thing, but coming up with truly innovative products and services was quite another. These managers also frequently expressed their frustration at seeing their companies and industries locked into traditional paradigms, with no sense of how and whether to move into new, innovative product and service realms. In the plaintive words of one manager, "When will we cease to be e-coolies?"[6]

The desire to go beyond "renting out IQ" to "start creating IP" (intellectual property) is becoming widespread in India's successful IT industry. Consider Infosys, perhaps India's best-known firm. Microsoft and Infosys commenced commercial operations about five years apart, in 1975 versus 1981, respectively. Yet Microsoft's fiscal year 2010 revenues were $62 billion, with profits of $19 billion, while Infosys barely managed to top $4 billion in revenues and $1 billion in profits. This disparity reflects fundamental differences in their business models: whereas Microsoft has incessantly focused on developing innovative products, Infosys has focused on services. It is not as though Microsoft's programmers are from another planet—a significant percentage of them are of Indian descent. Even iconic Indian firms such as Infosys now recognize that the challenge is to move from "outsourced and made in India" to "imagined and owned in India."[7]

Yet we must also bear in mind that only a few decades ago, Japan and Korea were prematurely categorized as havens for low-cost production, incapable of innovation. The 2010 *BusinessWeek* ranking of the most innovative companies in the world shows the fallacy of this prediction, with Toyota ranked at five, LG Electronics at seven, Sony at ten, Samsung at eleven, Nintendo at twenty, and Hyundai at twenty-two![8] Is it really all that far-fetched to imagine that the 2020 rankings could contain a significant number of Indian companies (beyond the Tata Group, already there at seventeenth) among the most innovative? Could "Made in India" become synonymous with innovation?

We spent four years trying to answer these questions, by investigating whether India could change from being the favored destination for offshore services to a locus of innovation. With its systematic, research-based approach, this book is the result of (1) more than fifty in-depth face-to-face interviews with CEOs, scientists, engineers, policy makers, and industry observers; (2) analyses of data on more than three hundred projects from surveys and internal company records to learn how globally distributed work is managed; (3) textual analyses of nearly one thousand media articles; and (4) statistical analyses of more than three decades' worth of patent data associated with inventors in India.[9] Unless otherwise indicated, the quotations in this book are from the aforementioned interviews we conducted during our research.

"Indians Don't Do Innovation"

At the beginning of this research project in 2007, when we posed the question "Can India do for innovation what it has already done for services?" to executives in both Western and Indian companies, we often received a dismissive response: Indians simply do not "do innovation." Usually, this scoff effectively terminated the conversations. Some executives more politely, though no less equivocally, asserted that "Indians make good programmers and accountants but can't do the creative stuff." Occasionally, this contention took on a veneer of sophistication, with the argument that it was the "regimented and rote-based Indian educational system" that was really responsible for killing creativity.

Yet Indians emerging from the Indian educational system often fire up the "innovation engine" of Silicon Valley. An entire book is even dedicated to describing *Silicon Valley Greats: Indians Who Made a Difference to Technology and the World.*[10] Some estimates suggest that Indians have founded more engineering and technology companies in the United States in the past decade than have immigrants from Britain, China, Taiwan, and Japan combined.[11] In addition, of all the immigrant firms founded during this period in the United States, 26 percent included at least one person of Indian descent as a founder.[12] Similarly, many of the most technologically sophisticated companies in the United States, such as Google, Microsoft, Cisco, Adobe, McAfee, and even NASA, have a significant percentage of Indians staffing their research-and-development (R&D) operations and innovation labs—disproportionately large relative to the percentage (about 1 percent) of Indians in the overall U.S. population. Indians have founded iconic Silicon Valley firms such as Sun Microsystems (Vinod Khosla) and Hotmail (Sabeer Bhatia) and helped invent key technologies such as Ethernet (Kanwal Rehki), fiber optics (Narinder Kapany), and the Pentium chip (Vinod Dham). Critically, these successful immigrant Indians in high-technology sectors are often those who succeeded in the "regimented and rote-based" educational system back in India.[13]

Impressed by their Indian talent in the United States, an increasing number of multinational corporations (MNCs), including those headquartered in Silicon Valley, have set up R&D operations in India. In 1985, Texas Instruments became the first major technology MNC to establish an R&D facility in Bengaluru. Since then, many other firms have followed suit, at an escalating pace. Cisco Systems placed its second global R&D headquarters in Bengaluru to leverage India's engineering resources and develop products for emerging markets. India is also the Yahoo! base for product and service development aimed at emerging markets. AstraZeneca, General Electric (GE), Intel, Microsoft, and Google all have global R&D centers in India. Estimates vary widely, but a NASSCOM 2010 study counted 750 R&D subsidiaries of MNCs employing over 400,000 professionals in India.[14] Considering that the historical practice for R&D centers has been to locate in the country in which the MNC is headquartered, this figure is remarkable. It also succinctly demonstrates the faith that these MNCs have in Indian talent and in India as a destination for innovation.

Although the absolute number of patents in the U.S. patenting system originating from India (i.e., patents with at least one inventor with an Indian address) remains much lower than the deluge of patents representing the United States, Japan, Germany, and the United Kingdom, the growth rates suggest a changing story. The number of patents filed by Indian authors or assignees in the U.S patent regime between 1995 and 2008 (4,861 patents) was eleven times greater than that between 1976 and 1994 (435).[15] In 2010, while total applications under the International Patent Cooperation Treaty rose 5.7 percent, those originating in India increased by 36.6 percent.[16] Another study of international patent applications from the United States showed that the contribution of inventors with Indian-heritage names (Patel and Singh being the most common) increased to 13.7 percent from 9.5 percent of international patent applications between 1998 and 2006.[17] None of these facts sits well with the notion that "Indians just don't do innovation."

At an even more fundamental level, the notion that innovation is alien to the Indian context is utterly foreign to our understanding of the business and, indeed, social life of India. Creativity is more than desirable in India; it is an absolute necessity in a country that is capable of generating an enormous range of constraints—social, economic, and technological—on individual action. The practice of finding fixes, workarounds, and shortcuts is a way of a life in India, so ubiquitous that it has even generated a colloquial sobriquet: *jugaad*, loosely translated as "making do" or improvisation.[18]

Even those with no interest in business or technology find it difficult to remain ignorant of the large numbers of Indian successes in creative fields such as literature, academia, advertising, and movies. For example, Indian authors writing in English have won global accolades for their literature, creative Indian advertising regularly earns awards at the Cannes Lions International Advertising Festival, and India is home to the world's largest movie industry. In academia, it seems rare *not* to find a smattering of Indian names on the table of contents of a top research journal.

India Inside: "Invisible" Innovation and Plan of the Book

As we made progress with our research, we realized that it is indeed difficult to point to Indian Googles, iPods, and

Viagras, because they do not exist—at least not yet. Instances of products and services being invented in India for consumers around the world are few, if any. But this perspective is too constraining for an understanding of innovation. As the economist and political scientist Joseph Schumpeter famously pointed out, in its essence, *innovation is novelty in how value is created and distributed*. It could entail new products or services, new methods of production, or indeed novel forms of organizing industries and firms.[19] In each case, we acknowledge that raw creativity alone is insufficient; knowledge of demand and the technology of production as well as execution capacity are also necessary ingredients. However, *there is no reason whatsoever why we should restrict the beneficiaries of innovation to be end consumers*, which is what we implicitly do when we ask where the Indian Googles, iPods, and Viagras are. Taking this broader conceptualization of innovation leads to an entirely different conclusion about innovation in India.

In our research, we uncovered substantial innovation taking place in India, but of a form that we did not anticipate: it is invisible to consumers around the world. It led us to develop figure 1-1 to help conceptualize what is happening in India with respect to innovation for the world. Specifically, four types of innovations originating from India remain invisible to end consumers around the world and have been a decade in the making:

1. *Globally segmented innovation* led primarily by major multinational corporations that have set up "captive" innovation and R&D centers in India. In chapter 2, we show that GE's John F. Welch Technology Centre and Intel's Indian operations in Bengaluru have already demonstrated that India can be a platform for generating innovation for global markets.

These companies have developed global products from their Indian R&D centers, just as the companies have done in their R&D centers in the West. At GE, one in six technologists worldwide is now part of the firm's 4,300-strong research facility in Bengaluru. Intel also launched its Xeon 7400 series in 2008, the first chip wholly designed and developed out of its Bengaluru center.

2. *Outsourcing innovation to Indian firms* where R&D services are provided on contract to support new product development for consumers in the developed world. In chapter 3, we discuss Indian companies that offer innovation as a service and that have helped

FIGURE 1-1

Visible and invisible innovation

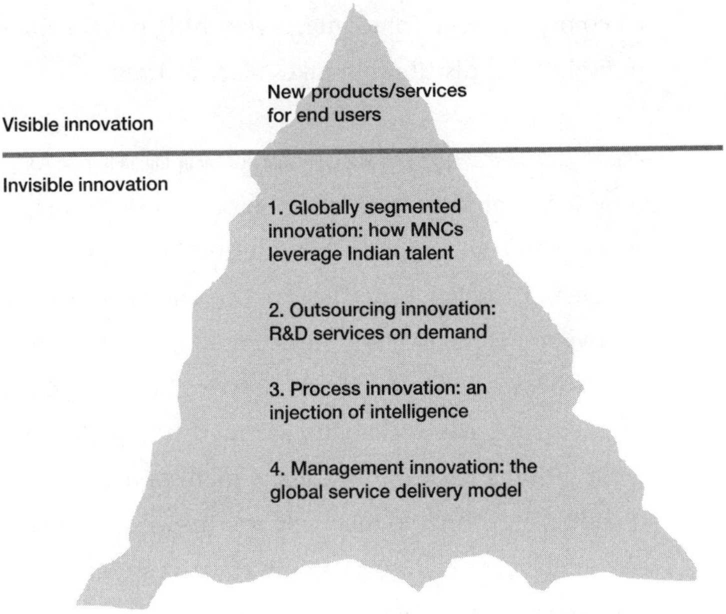

Visible innovation

New products/services for end users

Invisible innovation

1. Globally segmented innovation: how MNCs leverage Indian talent

2. Outsourcing innovation: R&D services on demand

3. Process innovation: an injection of intelligence

4. Management innovation: the global service delivery model

make offshore R&D services an estimated $20 billion
market in 2012. Companies such as Wipro Technologies, HCL Technologies, and Dr. Reddy's Laboratories
have convinced major MNCs to outsource parts of
their product development and R&D processes, from
semiconductors to drug discovery, to India. For example, HCL Technologies was heavily involved in the
development of Boeing's 787 Dreamliner, for which
HCL designed two mission-critical systems: one to
avert airborne collisions and another to enable land-
ings in zero visibility. According to Ian Q. R. Thomas,
president of Boeing India, the company found what
it needed in India: "In theory, we could place the
work anywhere. We're here because we found a level
of sophistication."[20] While this innovative work is
delivered in response to somebody else's specifications, it is technically complex, the IP generated may
be co-owned, and, sometimes, everything but the final
branding and distribution takes place in India.

3. *Process innovation through an injection of intelligence* by Indian firms. As
opposed to product innovation, process innovation
pertains to how a product is made and how new
products are developed. Chapter 4 reveals that process
innovation is increasingly surfacing in the Indian industry because of a phenomenon we call the *injection
of intelligence*. The availability of low-cost, high-skilled
labor in India has led to the assignment of overqualified personnel to relatively routine jobs, which
sometimes results in surprisingly effective process
innovations, even in what were previously considered

mature or low-tech settings. Ultimately, some of these process innovations become embedded in products marketed to the world. For instance, though 24/7 Customer began as a traditional call center company, it now develops various analytical tools that enable it to conduct predictive modeling, such that the firm can anticipate what a customer is calling about before the agent even answers the call. This process rests at the heart of a suite of products offered under the iLabs umbrella. Similarly, DenuoSource, in the course of a client engagement for IT services, saw an opportunity to convert a systematic approach to identifying store locations into a product called Location Analyzer. This "productization" that originates in process innovations is likely to be an important force for transforming invisible innovations into visible ones.

4. *Management innovation of the global delivery model* to effectively bring global scale and cost efficiencies to previously locally clustered service processes. Chapter 5 examines this, perhaps the most invisible of Indian innovations—the global service delivery model (hereafter referred to as the global delivery model). While the model is typically invisible to end consumers (except in the case of call centers), it is also, paradoxically, highly visible to most Western citizens because it is responsible for making the Indian outsourcing industry the success that it is today. The model is not a product or a process innovation but rather a management innovation, a new way of managing globally distributed work. For some observers, it is as significant as Henry Ford's assembly line model,

the total quality management movement, or DuPont's multidivisional form of organization. The global delivery model reconceptualizes formerly physically collocated activities by breaking them up into subtasks that can be handled in different geographical locations, and it specifies the necessary means for reintegrating this work. Such a model, however, is not easy to implement, as many later adopters have learned, because of the complex coordination problems inherent in this structure.

If the innovation embodied in products and services for end consumers represents the visible tip of the innovation iceberg, our research suggests that India is already significantly involved in the large, invisible, submerged portion. Despite touching the daily lives of consumers in the developed world, many Indian innovations are not conspicuous as being Indian. Intel ensures that end consumers know they are using a personal computer powered by "Intel Inside," but there is no "India Inside" label on products that embed innovations originating in India. Even if no single Google, iPod, or Viagra were to ever emerge from India, the invisible innovations outlined above already have significant implications for companies and policy makers in the developed world.

Yet, for us, "India Inside" describes the current state of the field, not necessarily its steady state. We ask what it would take for firms to build visible Indian innovation, in terms of products and services branded for global end users. Such visible innovation undoubtedly has powerful brand-building effects for both India and its companies. As many Indian policy makers remarked in our interviews, building globally visible products is almost a matter of national pride to demonstrate that India has arrived on the global economic stage.

Chapter 6 demonstrates a new class of innovative products that build on what is essentially a meta-process innovation—*frugal engineering*—to develop products for the budget-constrained Indian consumer. A large segment of India's population is both demanding and budget constrained. Meeting the needs of this segment today—the Nano car from Tata Motors is a prominent example—may lead to some new products that eventually diffuse to the West. While other observers have described these instances of "reverse innovation" in much detail, we focus on the underlying frugal engineering practices that collectively constitute a second-order innovation in the very process of designing and commercializing innovations.

Figure 1-1 is not meant to indicate a natural progression through which every company must pass and climb toward the top. While invisible innovations may help to build a thriving regime of visible innovations from India, the paradox is that for individual companies, the transition from business models built around invisible innovations to those based on visible innovations may be neither possible nor necessary. The captive R&D units we encounter in chapter 2 are part of an R&D network that is segmented both vertically and horizontally, and as long as this system of organizing work is in place, it will probably never generate innovations that are entirely produced in India (or anywhere else, for that matter). Even when the R&D services companies of chapter 3 (e.g., Dr. Reddy's Laboratories, Wipro) possess the capabilities to engage in new product development for global consumers, the companies may not have the incentives to do so. Companies such as 24/7 Customer and DenuoSource, profiled in chapter 4, are closely tied to the business-to-business (B2B) space because of their heritage, and rightly so. Therefore, the transition from invisible to visible innovation is unlikely and perhaps ill-advised for such companies.

Instead, the skills and capabilities built among these champions of invisible innovation may *indirectly* help incubate visible innovation efforts—through the movement of employees, spin-offs, new ventures, and the creation of a supportive ecosystem. Economists refer to these as *spillover effects*. In 2009, Ajay Pande, vice president of engineering at Adobe Systems, described the impact of Indian innovation at Adobe: "A large fraction of Adobe's products and their global impact is driven by technologists and business professionals from India. The learning and entrepreneurial opportunities this provides means that we are developing a talented set of business and technology leaders who will be at the forefront of creating great technology businesses from India in the future."[21]

Chapter 7 acknowledges and analyzes several significant constraints that are, at the very least, irritants and, at the most, significant impediments to India's potential to become an important innovation engine of the world. While the country obviously has a long way to go toward improving its basic infrastructure and eradicating poverty, these are not the issues we focus on. Constraints such as these have not prevented undisputed global leaders in the software development and back-office services from emerging in India. A sophisticated technology sector can coexist, perhaps unfortunately, with abject poverty. Further, in the world of international business, average firms from each country do not compete with one another, but the exceptional ones do and the number of innovations per capita matters less than the number of innovations. Thus, the traditionally weak performance of India on innovation indices that feature the population (or some correlate) in the denominator seem to tell us too little. We focus instead on three issues: the real talent pool, intellectual property protection, and venture financing.

In 2020, the median age in India will be twenty-eight, compared with thirty-seven in China, thirty-eight in the United States, forty-five in Western Europe, and forty-nine in Japan. Paradoxically, though the wealth of human capital implicit in this demographic dividend is a basis for optimism about Indian innovation, there is a real danger that this optimism is based on a *mirage of mighty labor pools*. With a few prominent but unrepresentative exceptions like the Indian Institutes of Technology (IITs), the country is still far from creating an infrastructure that can pump out the high-quality talent that will be necessary to make India synonymous with globally visible innovation. Indian companies and captive units certainly are pursuing several creative strategies to overcome these challenges, including the use of returning overseas Indians (repats) as a talent pool and backward integration into education through the adoption of schools and universities. However, these strategies cannot absolve the government of its responsibilities to fix the failures of the Indian schooling and university education systems.

India became a full participant in the TRIPS (Trade-Related Aspects of Intellectual Property Rights) Agreement in 2005, but companies still have legitimate concerns about the protection of their IP rights. These concerns have not deterred Indian R&D subsidiaries of MNCs from engaging in developing significant IP—in creating their own internal IP regimes. This, however, does entail additional costs and may deter some MNCs from leveraging India's innovation capabilities.

Finally, the ecology to support new entrepreneurial ventures in India is still nascent. Recent years have seen the emergence of new networks of angel investors and dedicated venture funds as the global financial community is becoming increasingly aware of the gap between the availability of venture capital and the existence of opportunity in India. Firms and individuals in India are finding creative ways of overcoming these constraints to innovation, even as much remains to be done.

The Emerging Innovation Challenge to the West

We believe that India's emergence as a global innovation hub has important implications for the developed world. But, even if it sells books, we do not wish to engage in scaremongering by contending that the rise of India (in concert with China) will lead to the inevitable decline of the West. Just as British and French living standards continued to rise throughout the 1900s—despite the twentieth century's being called the American century—the rise of India and China can be associated with growth in the developed world. But because the relative economic positions may change, both Western MNCs and policy makers will need smart responses to address the emerging innovation challenge by India. While the goal of the book is not to provide all the answers, but is to raise the important questions, we will not only provide a detailed look at the various kinds of innovation happening in India, but also end each chapter with a set of recommendations for MNCs, policy makers, and Indian companies. Those recommendations are specific to the kinds of innovation we discuss, but an overview of the implications for western MNCs and policy makers follows here.

The Challenge for Western MNCs

Let us consider the implications for MNCs first. By definition, such companies are not particularly anchored in their country of origin or the country they are headquartered in. If the locus of certain kinds of innovation shifts to India, one can be fairly sure that this is where the MNCs will be doing more of their innovative work. However, this also means that these organizations will confront some new internal stresses and strains.

Sinking skill ladders.

Consider the problem of sinking skill ladders. A *skill ladder* in a particular career or profession implies that to do highly sophisticated, innovative work, a person must have engaged in less sophisticated work in the earlier stages of his or her career. Few firms recruit a recent university graduate to handle their high-value-adding activities; rather, new entrants must work their way up each rung of the ladder. A person cannot become a partner in a consulting firm without having been an associate. Nor can an investment banker do so without first serving as an analyst. A professor must first be a student, and the head of a clinical research team must first be a research assistant. In each case, the junior people's contributions are valuable but often fully separable from the work of senior people. Yet the senior staff members know exactly what their juniors do, because of the seniors' previous experience as juniors. Without such knowledge, the seniors arguably cannot do their own jobs effectively—including making use of inputs from juniors.

The increasing use of Indian R&D centers by the most innovative MNCs in the world, at least to do highly vertically segmented work (i.e., developments far removed from the consumer), implies that this ladder now extends to India. Because the lowest rungs of the skill ladders for many innovation-related jobs are grounded in countries outside the West, the ladder has been fractured over geography. How can companies get the steady supply of people for the higher rungs if the lower rungs of the skill ladder are in a different geography? This problem is not merely an issue of getting people to move across countries (from India to wherever in the developed world the MNC is headquartered), though that in itself is complicated enough, especially considering the modern immigration policies of most Western economies. Rather, the act of moving the lower end of a skill ladder to an India or a China can be self-perpetuating. With the lower rungs on the ladder moved out of the West (or now less remunerative), Western university students are less likely to opt to invest in climbing those first few rungs. The limited availability of students in turn reinforces moving the lower rungs of the skill ladder offshore, and so on.

To be clear, we are not likely to hear a great sucking sound in Silicon Valley. That is highly unlikely. Nor are the R&D centers of global technology- and science-based companies in the West likely to shut down tomorrow.[22] But the hardware or pharmaceutical company deciding whether to open a new R&D lab in New Jersey or Basel will increasingly need to justify why not Bengaluru or Hyderabad, where technology specialists are relatively plentiful and cheaper. Thus, the locations where MNCs choose to develop their innovation capabilities in the future may change dramatically relative to today's received wisdom.

The "browning" of the top management teams.

Although decisions to locate innovation capacities in India may not by themselves cause problems for MNCs—whose very existence depends on a global mentality rather than a commitment to a particular geography—these decisions increasingly shift MNCs' location and composition of top management eastward. Perhaps this move is only natural: if both the growth markets and the talent are increasingly located in countries like India and China for MNCs, then why should the political center of gravity of Western MNCs be elsewhere? The challenge for Western MNCs lies in rapidly adapting their internal organizations to a new locus of innovation and growth. This may change the very fabric of these organizations and, more and more, the ethnicity of their leadership. Simply put, few of the MNCs that see innovation as their competitive advantage can escape the inevitable "browning" of their top management teams (TMT). Invisible innovation in India, combined with the increasing importance of China and India as markets, will demand governance innovations at MNCs.

The Challenge for Policy Makers in the Developed World

During the post–World War II period of prosperity for the developed world, the political deal in the United States was an acceptance of an open and flexible economy for increased income levels and full employment. In Europe, people accepted higher taxes in return for a larger welfare state that guaranteed free access to health care, education, and a minimum standard of living. Over the past two decades, though, these social contracts have been unraveling. The ability of the United States to generate full employment and deliver improving living standards has stalled, while Europe can no longer afford to keep its promises to the citizens.

The question of how the rise of the two Asian giants—India and China—will affect Western economies has captured the imagination of vast numbers of writers, politicians, academics, and pundits. The dilemma is to maintain, and perhaps even increase, the high standards of living of Western populations against low-cost labor competition from China, India, and the rest of the world. The pundits' answer, sooner or later, reverts to the argument that the developed world must sustain its dominant advantages in creative, innovative, and high-value-added work. This book argues that these advantages will increasingly be neither dominant nor easy to sustain. Of course, the loss of dominance does not preclude coexistence.

So what should policy makers in the West do? We see three broad categories of possible responses. First, developed countries could adopt increased protectionism by restricting offshoring in technology-intensive sectors, curbing immigration to minimize the transfer of jobs from current citizens to visiting foreigners, and excluding foreign students from graduate scholarships at Western universities. Not only would such actions essentially mean an opportunistic retraction of free trade and open democratic systems preached by the post–World War II developed world, but the economic benefits of this course of action are increasingly dubious in a global economy.

Even at a pragmatic level, protectionism is not a useful game to play when the growth opportunities are no longer in your own backyard. China and India are large enough to drive growth from their own domestic market and other emerging markets. If anything, Western governments should be citing their own track record of relatively nonprotectionist policies to pressure policy makers in India and China to reciprocate. For instance, Western MNCs will undoubtedly face new multinational competitors emerging from India as similar competitors emerged from Korea and Japan. These Indian competitors will have the advantage of leveraging a vast and rapidly growing domestic market. As these Indian MNCs seek to acquire companies around the world, Western MNCs will face competition on their home turf. But perhaps Western policy makers can seize the opportunity to ask India and other emerging economies to be as open to inward acquisition as the United States and the United Kingdom are.

Second, Western nations could attempt to beat countries like India and China at their own game. From what in a historical perspective is a twinkling of an eye, there has been a reversal of cultures between the East and the West. Travelers who frequent both the Western and the Eastern Hemispheres cannot fail to feel the differences in energy and ambition between the developed world and emerging markets. This is in startling contrast to the stereotypes that prevailed a mere decade or two ago—that Western economies and cultures were based on what the German sociologist and political economist Max Weber termed the *Protestant ethic*, which included the unabashed pursuit of wealth, ambition, and growth. In contrast, the East, based on Hindu and Buddhist spirituality, was characterized by a Zen-like existence that implied living in harmony with nature and repudiating materialism. The sustained prosperity of the West seems to have resulted in a negative view of consumption and sometimes even ambition. It is in China, India, and Vietnam today where one observes the hunger for wealth, rising consumption, ambition, entre-preneurialism, and a strong desire to work exceptionally hard to achieve economic outcomes.[23]

Recognizing this apparent reversal in cultures, the pages of elite periodicals such as *The Economist*, the *Financial Times*, and the *New York Times* have targeted Western policy makers and corporate leaders with editorials urging investments in the education systems, engaging more students in the science and technology curricula, and promoting the hard work ethic among the young. By embracing such changes, this perspective claims that the West can continue its lead in innovation and deliver rising living standards for its populations. There is undoubtedly merit in this advice, but the struggle to retain prosperity may simply not be as energizing as the hunger to achieve it. A letter to the editor of the *New York Times* highlights the issue:

> The one thing that pundits, columnists, politicians and economists would do well to remember is that the vast majority of any population of people are not bold visionaries devising "new services, new opportunities and new ways." Whether it is doctors or ditch-diggers, the vast majority of people just want to make an honest wage for an honest day's work and go home to their families.
>
> They do not want to work 120 hours a week devising the new "thing." They do not want to "invent smarter ways to do old jobs, energy-saving ways to provide new services, new ways to attract old customers or new ways

to combine existing technologies." The cold reality is that even if everyone shared this desire, most would not be able to succeed at it.

Are those that fail simply left to starve? Are those that fail somehow less human? Are those that fail somehow less American? If the answers that Mr. [Thomas] Friedman and his sources provide are correct then we Americans as a nation have larger problems than whatever is coming from the cheap and industrious engineers in Bangalore.[24]

In his 2011 State of the Union address, President Obama tried to create a "Sputnik moment" such as in 1957, when Russian entry into space unleashed large, publicly funded American research projects that ultimately led to many innovations. However, the rise of China and India is a slow and steady one rather than a galvanizing moment such as Sputnik. Furthermore, unlike the space race, where competition with the Russians was the dominant framework, today's situation brings ambiguity as to whether the West should compete or collaborate with China and India.

There is a third option: if you can't beat them, join them. This entails accepting the tremendous surge in innovation capacities in countries such as India and China. The key questions then revolve around how the Western economies can benefit from this surge. As with any strategic analysis, the right place to start is with distinctive competitive advantages. World-class universities and generous publicly funded science (including research in the defense and space sectors) continue to be a combination unique to the Western economies. India and China might eventually create the next Harvard, Massachusetts Institute of Technology, Oxford, or NASA, but they have not done so yet. Not only do countries like India and China suffer a dearth of world-class universities today, but the all-important linkage between universities and industry, so central to innovation in the West, is critically missing as well. Cultivating these linkages and fostering the growth of innovation clusters around universities—as has happened organically in Silicon Valley—has never been as important as it is today for the Western economies. This may be the most powerful instrument available to the West to retain cutting-edge innovation onshore.

At least one piece of the strategy to retain the Western strengths in innovation thus seems brutally obvious to us. Regardless of the financial difficulties of most Western economies, this is not the time to cut back on investment in public science and universities. In his 2011 State of the Union address, Barack Obama recognized the necessity of this investment: "Our free enterprise system is what drives innovation. But because it's not always profitable for companies to invest in basic research, throughout history our government has provided cutting-edge scientists and inventors with the support that they need. That's what planted the seeds for the Internet. That's what helped make possible things like computer chips and GPS."[25] He reiterated this point in another speech: "Even as we have to live within our means, we can't sacrifice investments in our future. If we want to win the future, America has to out-build, out-educate, out-innovate and out-hustle the rest of the world."[26]

Indeed, if the capacity at such world-class universities in the West could be expanded, coupled with a selective easing of immigration of the best students from around the world (not necessarily every applicant in a particular domain), there would be winners on both sides of the bargain. Policy makers should consider making it easier, not harder, for highly skilled and talented migrants to enter Western countries and contribute to onshore innovation capacity. As a complementary approach, Western educational institutions can help build the educational infrastructure in India, and many are now moving to do exactly this as the education sector has finally been liberalized to allow easier entry by foreign universities. The first overall message for Western policy makers is simple—invest in science and technology research and education in universities, and selectively promote immigration in these areas.

Paradoxically, Western policy makers may also consider making it easier for corporations to locate innovative activities in India, because today's innovation is bifurcating in two very different directions. The West may continue to hold on to its advantages at innovation arising from publicly funded basic science. In contrast, industrial innovation that can be globally segmented and outsourced, or is driven by budget-constrained consumers and budget-conserving talent, cannot be monopolized anymore. Countries like India and China are likely to dominate in this area. Thus, while the next pharmaceutical blockbuster, like a Viagra, might not emerge from India in the next few years, we do not see any reasons why the next iPods or Googles cannot. Allowing Western MNCs to locate innovation in these countries may give Western policy makers an opportunity to share in their gains from exploiting the next hot spot for innovation. Thus, the second message is equally simple: recognize that for certain kinds of innovation, the locus will inevitably and speedily shift eastward. Western policy makers should focus on benefiting from this shift, while strengthening the capacities at the kind of innovation that has a better chance of continuing to flourish in the West, for instance, innovation that is not easily segmentable and is closely linked to basic science.

India's Innovation Journey

A scenario in which India's innovation journey fizzles out before it sizzles is also possible, but, we think, is not plausible. Despite ongoing challenges in India, the developments discussed in this book spell out one thing quite clearly: for certain kinds of innovation, the long-held monopoly of the developed world is over. This does not automatically imply a new, Eastern monopoly on innovation; nor can India ignore the strong competitor at its own doorstep—China. It does, however, mean a world in which the capacity for innovation per se will not distinguish the West from the East. And as a result, different Western countries and MNCs will have to adopt different responses, given the respective realities of their politics, economics, and organizations. But one thing is sure: India's invisible-innovation challenge will need a response. We attempt to provide several potential responses and recommendations in this book. Let us now take a closer look at innovation inside India.

2 Globally Segmented Innovation
How Multinational Companies Leverage Indian Talent

OR MANY FIRMS, developing new products for consumers around the world is the most visible manifestation of innovation—the real deal. It is one thing for firms to manage another firm's IT system or to field calls from its customers but quite another to conceptualize a new product or service offering and take the idea all the way from conception to sale. This latter notion is the kind of innovation that people have in mind when they ask, "Where are the Indian Googles, iPods, and Viagras?"

The problem with this perspective is that it virtually ignores innovation in the B2B space and how new-product development is currently conducted in MNCs. Today, the new-product development activities of MNCs are segmented across geographies, something we explain in more detail below, and consequently, much of this development is visible only in a B2B context. For example, most passengers neither know nor care where the aircraft engine inside the airplanes was designed and manufactured; most electricity consumers do not know which country came up with the wind turbines that generate their electricity; and few computer users—hardcore technophiles excluded—realize which country designed the microprocessor in their machines. The answer, in each case, could be India.

"We Helped Develop Everything I'm Talking About, Right Here"

We arrive at GE's John F. Welch Technology Centre to find a corporate campus that is large, modern, and stylish, with its own power and water treatment plants—a marvel of world-class infrastructure. But we have visited too many of India's new-economy firms in Bengaluru on prior research trips to be easily impressed. The man we meet is another matter.

Our first impression of Guillermo Wille is that we could well be dealing with a fellow academic. This assumption turns out to be correct; the donnish Wille holds a doctorate in power electronics and has taught at the University of Aachen. Our second impression is that he radiates a sense of powerful but understated pride in what surrounds him—that is, GE's

John F. Welch Technology Centre, which he has headed since 2001. As our conversation gets under way, he mentions a string of technological marvels: a transparent roof that spans three hundred meters without any central supports (made of a special polycarbonate, it spans the Shanghai South Railway station), a device to display integrated anatomical information from a CT scan with live functional information from a PET scan, a car bumper that self-destructs on impact (rather than destroying, say, the leg of an unlucky pedestrian), and a portable electrocardiogram that is slightly larger than a laptop (versus the traditional machine, which is about the size of a carry-on suitcase).[1] "We helped develop everything I am talking about, right here," he adds, almost as an afterthought. The markets for these wonder products are truly global, encompassing the United States, Europe, Asia, and, of course, India itself.

We feel a strong sense of déjà vu when we travel to Intel and meet Praveen Vishakantaiah, another scientist, who heads Intel's R&D center in Bengaluru, India. It is Intel's largest R&D unit outside the United States, having recently overtaken the much older Israeli unit. The Intel India Development Centre (IIDC) was established in 1998 with a $1 billion investment. Indian engineers at IIDC work on the design of chips and chip sets, reference designs, and system software and lead the development of chips for server and mobile technology markets around the world. The workforce had grown to about 2,500 people by 2009.

Some of this work is truly "blue-sky" research. For example, IIDC delivered the world's first experimental chip that is capable of one trillion operations per second (or one *teraflop*). As the world's first programmable processor, it aimed to deliver this teraflop performance for personal computers and servers, while using less energy than many single-core processors. Although the company has no plans to bring this exact chip to market, tera-scale research continues to pursue innovations in processor and core functionalities, as well as in the design of software that can best leverage multiple processor cores. In 2008, IIDC launched a new Xeon processor for use in high-end servers. This processor, the world's first six-core x86 processor, was designed at IIDC. Intel's chip code names tend to sound like Anglo-American suburbs, so it code-named the x86 Xeon chip Dunnington, but the joke among insiders was that it should have been called Dunn-in-India—because it was.

Srini Koppolu, who headed Microsoft's India Development Centre in Hyderabad, painted a similar picture. His group encompassed large teams of engineers who formulated and developed functionality for modules within major products (e.g., Windows), as well as smaller teams that work on end-to-end development of smaller products (e.g., one was under way in the radio-frequency identification space during our visit). Another Microsoft development, the Visual Studio Test, granted the team in India overall product responsibility. Working from Hyderabad, the Indian product manager led a team of about eighty people, of whom twenty members were located at Microsoft Redmond, and another twenty at Microsoft North Carolina.

During our research for this book, in addition to GE, Intel, and Microsoft, we visited and spoke with the leaders of "captive"—wholly owned subsidiary—Indian R&D units of companies such as AstraZeneca, EMC, Philips, Pfizer, and Alcatel-Lucent. Even as people question the notion that truly innovative product development can occur in India, these units are providing striking evidence that it can. Our research also revealed a dramatic increase in the U.S. patenting rate by MNC subsidiaries in India, which belies the notion that these developments have relevance only for the local Indian market (figure 2-1).[2] The increase is driven both by an increase in the number of R&D subsidiaries that patent and by an increase in patenting by each existing subsidiary. Patenting with the U.S. Patent and Trademark Office (USPTO) is a costly exercise, and Indian firms and subsidiaries do not undertake it lightly without expectation of gains outside India.

In many of the captive units we researched for this book, we found instances of truly novel and unique technology developments for global markets. Yet global consumers rarely recognize India as the country of origin, because most of this innovation takes place in the B2B context. When we refer to

FIGURE 2-1

U.S. patenting by subsidiaries of U.S. multinational corporations in India

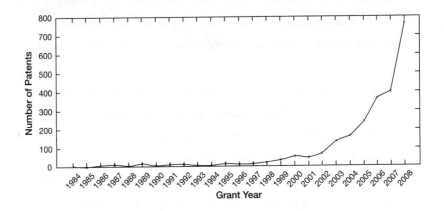

Source: Tufool Al-Nuaimi, Gerard George, and Phanish Puranam, *Emerging Economies as a Source of Innovation: Patenting by Indian and Chinese R&D Subsidiaries* (2011).

the B2B context, we do not necessarily mean only product or service markets in which the customers are firms, rather than individual consumers. Instead, we mean that the innovation occurring in these Indian captive units is visible only to other business units, whether within or outside the MNC, regardless of who purchases the final product.

To understand the nature of this invisibility, consider the idea of *segmenting* R&D activities—that is, breaking activities down into smaller parts that can be performed in different geographies. An obvious segmentation of R&D is vertical, into processes that capture customers' requirements, generate product specifications, search out technological solutions to meet the desired specifications, prototype the results, and then manufacture and sell the results of the process. This type of segmentation creates a strong sense of sequence: one process requires the preceding processes to have been conducted, if not completed. Another method is horizontal—a kind of segmentation that often arises from complex, multicomponent technologies, such as engines, IT hardware, or even complex software. The various components involved, in principle, could be developed in parallel, as long as the component interfaces support eventual assembly and interoperability (figure 2-2).

Now, either type of segmentation of R&D activities would make Indian contributions invisible to end consumers, even if the final product were a consumer product. With vertical segmentation, which is what most people intuit, the Indian R&D unit of an MNC might work to the specifications that another R&D or marketing unit in the United States designed. With horizontal segmentation, the Indian unit might contribute its specialist expertise to the development of one of the subsystems that constitute the final product. But because no country unit is solely responsible for the final result, it is difficult to associate any particular country with the innovation. Thus, Guillermo Wille at GE took great pains to state clearly that his unit in Bengaluru *helped develop* everything he mentioned, and he would not take sole credit for the aircraft engines and wind turbines that provide classic example of complex products with multiple subsystems and component technologies. But equally important, no other R&D unit in the GE network can claim sole credit, either! The segmentation of R&D efforts thus effectively wraps a cloak of invisibility around the innovation taking place in the R&D units of MNCs in India. It also makes the question "Where was it really innovated?" difficult to answer, if not outright irrelevant.

FIGURE 2-2

Vertical versus horizontal segmentation of global R&D projects

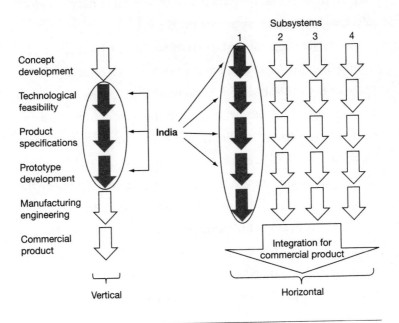

The global segmentation of R&D activities is just one example of the general principle of specialization based on country-specific advantages—a principle first articulated by Adam Smith and David Ricardo almost two centuries ago. So what advantages motivated companies such as GE, Intel, and Microsoft to bring their extremely sophisticated technology development work to India in the first place?

An Unavoidable Destination

In addition to governmental incentives or stipulations, the key factors that drive firms' locations of R&D operations, according to existing research, are proximity to an important market, access to technical talent in the labor force or academia, and a strong IP regime.[3] By this account (ignoring perhaps the access to high-quality talent), the presence of captive R&D units in India, with their mandate to help develop products for global markets, seems surprising.

The need to be close to the market to develop products or customize them to local tastes has historically been critical in India. Some of the earliest MNC R&D centers (e.g., Unilever) in India reflected this need. But in contrast to the previous emphasis on customizing Western products to Indian tastes and purchasing capacities, the R&D centers we encountered did not view this effort as their sole or even their primary mandate. Nor were the captive R&D units we visited isolated cases; many other captive R&D units, including those for Texas Instruments, Honeywell, Adobe, Cisco, Nokia, Ericsson, Samsung, and Google, have significant global market mandates, and media accounts imply that more are joining their ranks every week.

Firms also might locate an R&D unit in India if it is the "lead market," or a market that sets the standards and specifications eventually accepted in other markets. Increasingly, India is emerging as a lead market for certain innovations (we expand on this point in chapter 6). For example, some captive units have been established in India both for their proximity to the Indian market and in an attempt (eventually) to meet global demands. A case in point is AstraZeneca's R&D unit in Bengaluru; the unit focuses on tropical diseases. The benefits of this type of research accrue primarily to society, rather than to the corporate sponsor, so setting up this R&D unit in India was a sound economic decision, because the investment would be low, commensurate with the expected profits. Furthermore, AstraZeneca's research benefits patients all over the developing world, not just India.

It is also possible to view AstraZeneca's investment in India as an option. As Tanjore Balganesh, the head of research at AstraZeneca Bengaluru, pointed out, "You build an organization hoping ten years, twenty years, down the line, the principles of drug discovery are the same; all that will be needed is adding in a disease component as we move forward. So if you were to tell me tomorrow the Bengaluru unit should work on cardiovascular disease, it's a very small investment to change this into a cardiovascular unit." In other words, what AstraZeneca has built in India is the option to pursue future drug discoveries that can benefit the world by addressing disease areas relevant to not just the developing world but also developed countries.

Historically, though, a robust IP regime has not been India's strong suit. To encourage growth of the domestic drug manufacturing sector, the Indian government enacted the

Patents Act in 1970. The act denied composition patents for chemicals, foods, and drugs (though it permitted process patents), as well as all forms of patent protection for agricultural and horticultural products. The vast majority of patents (80 to 90 percent) at that time were held by foreigners, who were seen as intent on protecting their imports and depriving India of "goods at cheaper prices." Although the effect was most noticeable in the pharmaceutical industry, the regulation produced negative spillovers throughout India's economy in the form of a general lack of sophistication when it came to the importance of IP rights. Beginning in 1994, a series of amendments to the IP regime started with an acknowledgment of the need to move toward global patent standards (e.g., twenty years' protection for both products and processes in all sectors) and, in 2005, culminated in an effective harmonization of India's IP regime with the TRIPS standards. Yet how this regime will be implemented remains an open question.

At least for some companies (e.g., GE, AstraZeneca, Microsoft, Intel), concerns about IP regimes and the (lack of) sophistication of the domestic market are trumped by the attractiveness of the talent pool. The availability of high-quality talent is a key driver, as becomes evident within minutes of speaking to leaders of captive R&D units such as Wille and Vishakantaiah. Wille spoke to the importance of talent: "The engine behind GE's double-digit annual organic growth is talent. If you step back and think about the significant growth of the company, well . . . it wouldn't have been possible if we'd stayed only in the U.S. or Europe. Today, we have just over fifty-four hundred engineers and scientists in India. About 60 percent have advanced degrees, 20 percent have global experience. If you take a look through the company, about one out of six engineers works out of India. Soon it may be one in every four."

At GE's John F. Welch Technology Centre, the talent pool features sophisticated skills in computer science and mechanical and electrical engineering. Analytics and material sciences are considered strengths that enable the center to occupy a distinct niche in GE's segmented, global R&D network.

At least initially, though, the lower cost, rather than the depth of the talent pool, likely encouraged technology MNCs such as Texas Instruments and Intel to establish their R&D units in India. For example, commonly cited (though disputed) estimates show that India produces 350,000 engineers every year, compared with 70,000 in the United States.[4] But wages in India for comparable technical talent were a fraction of what they were in the United States or Europe at the beginning of the decade—though this gap is closing. In addition, most captive R&D units were initially doing a lot less "R" and rather more "D." Significant vertical segmentation also occurred, with the Indian units providing support and an "extended technical workbench" rather than leading the product development process.

However, over time, confidence in the capabilities of India's talent pool increased. Rick Steffens, who heads Hewlett-Packard's Systems Technology and Software division, exemplified this confidence as he spoke about HP's India R&D center: "As those teams started to get some experience . . . what we started noticing was that they were also capable of making changes to and enhancing the product."[5] When speaking of Microsoft's unit in India, Bill Gates recalled that Microsoft's research facility in India exceeded schedule expectations. This kind of talent makes India an "unavoidable destination" for R&D and innovation centers.

Keep Them Coming: Managing Talent, IP, and Connectedness

Talent may be what prompts MNCs to consider shifting the locus of their innovative work to India, but the talent pool is not infinite. When it comes to higher-level skills, the pool is actually frightfully shallow, as Rahul Bedi, a senior manager at Intel's IIDC, told us: "A couple of years ago, we put the number of silicon design engineers in the country at roughly twenty thousand . . . I'm sure those numbers would have grown in the years hence, but between Intel and a few peers, we take the lion's share of that talent. And if you're talking at the PhD level . . . I think about fifteen or sixteen PhDs in areas of our interest came out of the country in one year. That's not exactly a fantastic number."

Unlike the generic programming skills available on a large scale, on which India's IT industry is based, R&D requires more specialized skills. A similar problem afflicts the life sciences. Although AstraZeneca has about a hundred scientists involved in its tropical-diseases research unit in Bengaluru (around forty have doctoral degrees), the dearth of good medicinal chemistry expertise is already becoming apparent.

At Intel's IIDC, in particular, managers are also keenly aware of the weaknesses of the IP regime. As Vishakantaiah noted, "We've been paranoid about IP rights from day one. Why? Simple: with our first breach, it'd be, 'Thanks, nice knowing you guys,' and we'd be shut down. We'd be done before we even began." Furthermore, the weaker IP regimes in places such as India and China cause MNCs to segment their work related to innovative projects in such a way that minimizes the risk of any potential leakage.[6]

Underlying Vishakantaiah's statement is another dynamic that may help captive R&D units overcome the challenges of the Indian institutional context: the strong motivation to prove to the parent organization that India is a viable destination for R&D. The leaders of several R&D captive units, including those for Intel, Microsoft, and Alcatel-Lucent, were repatriated Indians who had previously worked in the parent organization in the United States. These "repats" felt a strong motivation to prove, both to themselves and to the parent organization, that their units could provide R&D work equal to global standards—a premise on which they might have based their return to India in the first place.

Srini Koppolu at Microsoft also argued that the "mother ship" experience is critical for helping integrate the captive unit in India into the parent, in spite of the challenges of time zones and geography:

It is important to have Microsoft-experienced people be part of this organization from the beginning. Basically, Redmond experience is critical; I won't say other parts of the world, but Redmond experience is critical. The credibility of those people that we get from Redmond is highly valued—to have at least a few people in key roles who have good credibility in the company—so that means they worked on some of these important major products, they've been through multiple release cycles, they have a decent kind of network, they're known to have been good, solid engineering managers—these are all important aspects.

In addition, all the senior managers from the Hyderabad unit make at least three to four trips a year to the United States, again with the goal of building connections.

The Quality of Globally Segmented Innovation: Evidence from a "Twin" Study

The growth in patenting activities by the captive R&D units of MNCs in India is one clear indicator of their success. But one may question the quality of the innovations that these patents represent. To understand how they compare with the quality of innovative activity in the R&D units in the West, one of us conducted a research study with our collaborators, Tufool Al-Nuaimi and Gerry George of Imperial College in London. We collected data on all successful USPTO patent applications in the semiconductor sector made by the top twenty-one Indian and Chinese subsidiaries of U.S. MNCs between 1989 and 2004. In the United States, firms in the semiconductor industry have a higher propensity to use patents to protect their innovations than do firms in other industries.

For each of the patents filed by an Indian or a Chinese subsidiary, we found a "twin"—a patent filed in the same year by the U.S. units of the same MNC, in the same specific technology area, with nearly the same number of inventors listed as authors on the patent. For these pairs of twins, we calculated the number of times they had been cited by patents filed after them—a commonly used metric of their impact. We found that on average, the offspring of the U.S.-based units were cited more by later patents filed by competitors and other firms than were their twins from Indian and Chinese subsidiaries. However, the twins were indistinguishable in terms of the number of times they were cited by later patents filed by R&D units within the same MNC (which could be anywhere in the world). At least within the MNC, the impact of the innovations created by the Indian and Chinese subsidiaries seems to be comparable to that created by their U.S counterparts working on very similar problems. The higher overall impact of the patents filed by the U.S units is driven by citations filed by geographically proximate competitors and other firms. It is well known that knowledge "spills over" locally, and there just happen to be many more competitors for these semiconductor firms located in the United States than in India and China.[7]

Interestingly, we also found that the patents from the Indian subsidiaries on average were cited more often than the Chinese subsidiaries. This resonates with the results of a broader study one of us conducted with Suma Athreye of Brunel University.[8] For every patent granted within the USPTO between 1976 and 2006, we examined those that had at least one author resident in India or China. There, too, we found that Indian patents typically receive more citations than do Chinese patents. A close examination reveals that the difference is largely driven by the subsample of patents filed by MNC subsidiaries patenting out of India and China. Put simply, MNCs appear to be producing innovations with higher impact (as measured by forward citations) in India than in China, and this effect is strong enough to make Indian patents as a whole appear to be more cited on average than Chinese patents in the USPTO. These results are consistent with anecdotal evidence that Chinese R&D subsidiaries of MNCs are primarily engaged in localized projects while Indian R&D subsidiaries are pursuing projects that are more global.

Made in India, Made by Indian Firms?

Surprisingly, the MNCs, rather than homegrown Indian firms, appear to be at the forefront of innovating in India for the world. New-product development for global markets is still relatively rare in Indian companies, though a few examples exist. The reasons for the rarity of these examples are identical to the problems that the MNC R&D units have needed to overcome to set up shop in India.

First, products rely on IP, and as we have noted repeatedly, India's IP regime has not offered robust protection for novel ideas. As a result, the risk-return ratio was simply not favorable to pursuing new-product development. As the Indian IP regime improves, and sophistication about protecting and managing IP increases, this may stimulate more attempts at product development.

Second, the domestic market has not traditionally been a lead market. For much of its postindependence history, India maintained a highly regulated and well-protected domestic market, which might have made global markets less interesting to the majority of Indian companies. Even companies that wanted to explore global markets realized that their experience with the unique Indian market was of little use. In particular, proximity to the market drives product development success, and for most Indian companies, the market was not noted for its sophistication or purchasing power. This characterization also is beginning to change. For example, Infosys, one of India's premier software companies, sells Finacle, a software solution that provides the "software guts" for a bank branch, with which all other applications interface. The core of the product is a solution that Infosys first developed for an Indian bank in 1993. Along with a handful of other such products (e.g., i-Flex), Finacle represents an example of product development for global markets by an Indian company. Interestingly, i-Flex and Finacle have become global leaders in the banking technology space.[9]

Third, Indian firms face formidable challenges in gaining insights into global customers. Regardless of whether a captive R&D unit is vertically or horizontally segmented, it enjoys mechanisms already in place to link its development process to deep knowledge of the end market (often in the developed world). Domestic firms have difficulty replicating such access to global customer insights. Interestingly, IT services companies, which have had to learn to work with their customers across geographies, may have advantages at solving this problem. Consider Infosys's Magic Mirror, launched in 2007. Magic Mirror was a joint effort with Motorola, Paxar (which provided the RFID readers), and thebigspace, a boutique retail designer that specializes in consumer interaction technologies (which provided the design).

The Magic Mirror is a real mirror designed for fitting rooms in retail clothing stores, but it also features a sensor that detects which items customers have brought into the room. With this information, the mirror provides customers with more than a simple reflection; they can access information about the items they have in hand, receive tips on other clothing and accessories that match their chosen outfit, and summon a clerk to bring a different size. The retailer then takes the information from the mirror to track consumers' buying patterns, recommend cross-sales, and prevent theft. Infosys's "smart visual merchandising software" supports thebigspace's specialist technologies. In this case, creative partnering strategies overcome the challenges associated with gaining insights into lead markets that are halfway around the world.

Fourth, new-product development is typically characterized by deferred and risky returns. When Indian companies exploit their enormous labor cost advantages to deliver services to a global market, they may ignore new-product development activities that would provide lower risk-adjusted returns. Again, though, this calculus is changing as wage arbitrage advantages begin to erode. For example, in 2000, salaries of software programmers based in the United States were almost twenty times the salaries in India; today, we estimate that it is between five and nine times.[10] Lower-cost geographies like the Philippines are seeking to do to India what India has already done to the United States and Europe. In this context, new-product development suddenly makes more economic sense for Indian firms.

Fifth, Indian firms need to address the absence of management expertise necessary for global-caliber new-product development activities. For various reasons, some of which we have outlined previously, Indian companies have not developed internal competencies in new-product development for global markets. This situation, too, may be changing. Through imitation, competition, and talent migration, technical and management competencies will inevitably spill over from MNC units to their domestic counterparts. More than one hundred MNC R&D captive units reside in Bengaluru alone, and the average size of R&D captive units is about six hundred employees.[11] Surely, some of the skills these sixty thousand employees acquire will find their way into the broader ecosystem. This process would be similar to the rush of MNC subsidiary managers in India to family business houses in the early 1990s, in response to the economic liberalization and the consequent need to professionalize the Indian family firm.[12] When Indian firms need or desire to increase innovation, they have a talent pool at the captive R&D units of MNCs waiting to be tapped.

Recommendations

Inside many of the captive R&D units in India today are systematic innovation processes, as would appear in such units anywhere in the developed world. However, because of the global segmentation of R&D, much of this innovation remains hidden from global consumers. What does this imply for managers and policy makers?

- MNC perspectives on their innovation activities in India have changed in various ways:

    - MNCs see India as able to move from the localization of products for domestic market to developing products for global markets.

    - From having the India center develop a defined, small piece in the vertical segmentation of the innovation project, MNCs are now giving India complete responsibility for entire subsystems in the horizontal segmentation of an innovation project.

    - Beyond moving innovation projects to India because of cost savings, MNCs increasingly move to India to leverage the scale of talent available.

    - After decades of seeing India as a lagging market, in certain industries like telecommunications, MNCs now see India as the lead market in which to introduce new products and services.

- Western policy makers confident of keeping highly paid innovation jobs at home should be aware of several observations about Indian innovation:

  - Leading MNCs, including those at the cutting edge of technology in their respective industries, see India as an unavoidable destination for innovation for their markets worldwide.

  - The vertical and horizontal segmentation of innovation activity makes Indian contributions invisible, but just as the Indian units cannot claim sole credit for the final innovation, neither can any other R&D unit in the network.

  - MNCs with Indian innovation centers are observing fast migration to higher-valued-added projects at these centers; the evidence suggests that the quality of innovation generated by these centers may be no different from that created by the R&D units in the West working on similar problems.

  - Even as MNCs are restructuring R&D activities in the West, they are ramping up in India (setting up new centers and increasing the head count at existing centers).

- Indian companies attempting to develop new products for the world have to overcome six historical obstacles:

– Weak IP protection led Indian firms not to seek new-product development as a source of their competitive advantage.

– India was not a lead market for products and services, but was a follower of global trends.

– Gaining deep customer insight necessary for developing new products for faraway markets was not easy.

– It was easier for Indian firms to compete on cost rather than getting into the high-returns, high-risk new-product development game.

– There was limited availability of management expertise in India to manage global new-product development activities.

– Indian firms have substantial potential to improve innovation capability and overcome these obstacles via spillover effects from MNC innovation centers.

3 Outsou[rcing]
R&D Ser[vices]
on Deman[d]

ASK THE PROVERBIAL source on th[e]
name some companies at the glob[al]
front of technological innovation, an[d]
are likely to hear names such as AstraZenèca, Boeing, Cis[co,]
Ericsson, IBM, Novartis, Nortel, Motorola, Nokia, and Xerox.
However, few might realize the role of Indian companies in
the innovation processes of these global companies. MNCs
headquartered in the developed world are increasingly outsourcing their innovation (R&D, product development) processes to Indian firms.

What qualifies as true R&D outsourcing—a practice also
referred to as innovation on demand or innovation out-

sometimes difficult to determine, because the
is field feels nearly impenetrable. For example,
the label *R&D outsourcing* applies to the provi-
ic IT services, such as software development and
nce, testing, enterprise-level IT integration to R&D-
firms. At other times, it means the provision of IT
services to a client's R&D department. Our focus in
apter is on Indian companies that offer R&D services to
oduct development and R&D functions of their client
. Many Indian companies today are offering innovation
ices on demand in hardware design, drug development,
p design, consumer electronics, automotive services, and
binformatics, among other sectors.[1] R&D offshoring to In-
ia is expected to be worth 13 billion dollars in 2011, growing
at more than 10 percent per year.[2]

When Western companies outsource parts of their product
development processes to Indian companies, the innovative
work being done in India becomes doubly invisible, cloaked
by (at least) two corporate boundaries. In this chapter, we
examine this outsourcing-innovation phenomenon and the
paths by which it has become an increasingly important element in the Indian global services portfolio, together with
India's existing service strengths, such as IT, back-office, and
voice-based offerings.

In striking contrast with the popular view that Indian outsourcing reflects a cost-efficiency strategy applicable only to
routine and low-skill work, a closer look at examples of R&D
outsourcing for innovation reveals clearly that Indian third-
party centers (i.e., outsourcers) engage in significant product
innovation activities, even if their names never appear in the
final product's branding and marketing communications. In

particular, we examine the flourishing invisible innovations in both engineering and the life sciences, as well as what they mean for various stakeholders—clients, consumers, and even the outsourcers themselves—as they gather momentum.

Outsourcing Innovation Through R&D Services

Outsourcing innovation sounds rather like an oxymoron. The notion that a company would outsource elements of its innovation processes, often seen as being at the very core of its competitive advantage, sounds unorthodox. And if a company were to outsource elements of its R&D process, why would it select India, which is better known for its strengths in non-core-support functions, such as maintaining IT systems, running back offices, or answering customer calls? For insights into these questions, consider the case of Wipro Technologies.[3] As one of the top IT services companies, Wipro Technologies enjoys worldwide recognition and status as the flagship company of the Indian IT industry. However, even people familiar with the name are not likely to realize that the company also ranks as one of the world's largest independent R&D services providers. In 2009, about 30 percent of its revenues came from R&D services, flowing through its Product Engineering Services (PES) segment. In addition, Wipro has been successful in this R&D services market for nearly two decades.

In a very real sense, Wipro pioneered offshore outsourcing of R&D services to India. In the early 1980s, when it first entered the IT space, Wipro had a mandate to build IT systems for the Indian market, especially in the immediate aftermath of IBM's exit. When IBM left India, the floodgates opened to other firms that might develop lower-priced operating systems and applications for the domestic market. Of course, developing these applications was challenging; each application required obtaining source code from owners of the operating systems to ensure compatibility. Wipro wanted access to a standard operating system, but at the time, these were typically closed and proprietary. Rather than give up, Wipro initiated contact with major global technology companies, such as AT&T Bell Labs, Intel, and Motorola.

V. R. Venkatesh, a senior engineer at that time (and now senior vice president for Product Engineering Services), was part of this process of reaching out to proprietary operating system providers. The efforts, he noted, meant that Wipro "became known as the guys who were good at this stuff. Some of these companies then came back and said, 'Let's use Wipro's capabilities in this space.'" Wipro first began working formally as a service provider in the product engineering and R&D services area in 1993. NCR Corporations was an early client, and Nortel followed soon after, searching for a partner that could handle software development related to telecommunication switches.

Even in the early 1980s, prior to the information revolution, technology companies faced human resource constraints in their R&D activities; the level and scale of talent in India, and Wipro's ability to channel this talent, made the company attractive on two fronts. Venkatesh provided us with some context: "You have to remember that this was before the economic environment in India had opened up, and it was difficult for these players to consider setting up their own captive units. It would have been very hard for them to set up shop, hire people, know which were the good universities, and understand the regulatory environment in India. They came to us instead." But coming to Wipro still represented a leap of faith for these companies, said Venkatesh: "Trust was (and, of course, is) very important in these relationships. Remember, we are holding their IP, in some cases, before the IP rights regime had been changed in India [i.e., in 2005]."

Wipro's entry into the R&D services field owed as much to serendipity as it did to strategy, though. The capabilities that Wipro exploited to become a leading R&D services provider were largely based on its early desire to build technical expertise and thus serve the domestic, not global, market. But in gearing up to meet the technical demands of its domestic market (which never really materialized, anyway), Wipro gained a competitive advantage in the R&D offshoring industry. Specifically, even this early in the life of the industry, the company had become an expert in important technologies, built a robust talent pipeline, and earned the trust of its clients, even as it faced the challenges of operating in a weak IP regime.

Today, two types of projects account for the bulk of PES work at Wipro. First, in a more traditional model, Wipro serves as an extended R&D resource provider or offshore development center for clients. This model accounts for about two-thirds of the total outsourced offshore R&D services market in India. Wipro essentially staffs projects that clients define, manage, and control. However, these engagements often evolve into multiple and increasingly larger projects—the "onion-peel approach," in Venkatesh's words, for which "the engagement typically starts at the periphery and then moves inward into the products." The typical path for this approach would be something like the following: product development support work leads to applications (depending on the product), which lead to interfaces and applications, which lead to the kernel of the product (e.g., protocols, features, standards).

This onion-peel process often leads to the second model of engagement, the *end-to-end development* of a single product or product family. Such projects arise because a client has limited capacity and "bandwidth" (in terms of managerial and technical talent) to support a particular product it wants to develop. Wipro's goal for these projects is to handle most of the work in India, with a few people located at the client's site, as well as staged reviews when client employees visit the offshore site. However, the client retains the ultimate responsibility for testing, conforming to local regulations, and obtaining approvals.

Thus, even if Wipro initially gets the job for basic maintenance work, the company might eventually become the technical owner of a client product's entire life cycle. For example, a computer printer manufacturer wanted a new font compression technology that would apply to all its many printer product lines. Without the in-house resources to develop this technology, the client turned to Wipro's offshore development center in India. Wipro ultimately became the capability owner for this font compression technology and applied it to various products launched by the client.

The technical complexities in end-to-end development projects can be significant. The basic IP in these projects typically belongs to the client. However, Wipro might need to integrate other companies' or its own IP into a client's solution. In some of these cases, Wipro has the prebuilt IP that it can license to its clients, which also creates licensing revenue. For example, in the consumer electronics domain, Wipro has significant IP in the digital arena, not all of which is patented, but which includes prebuilt solutions in a particular domain. By developing IP that can be reused across clients in platform technologies, Wipro exemplifies one of the most significant ways that R&D services companies enhance their technical competence and benefit their clients. These service companies do not expect those clients to make that input known to end consumers, though.

This setting means that I. Vijaya Kumar, the chief technology officer of Wipro PES, faces a frequent (and annoying) question: Is Wipro doing "real R&D work," or is it just doing the lower-end portions of real R&D work? We suspect that these questioners have in mind an unsegmented, single-location R&D paradigm, which is swiftly becoming history. Today, R&D is segmented even *within* the boundaries of the global enterprise, as we pointed out in our chapter 2 discussion of captive R&D units in India. Using those terms, we can describe Wipro's business path as usually beginning with vertically segmented R&D work, but then later evolving into horizontally segmented work.

From Generics to Contract R&D

A possible explanation for the success of companies such as Wipro in R&D services is that the leap from writing code on demand to designing software or hardware to specification may not be that large. Could innovation on demand—delivered from India—work outside the confines of the IT sector? The answer, as exemplified by Dr. Reddy's Laboratories, is a resounding yes. Dr. Reddy's Laboratories (DRL) is a leading Indian pharmaceutical company known for developing, manufacturing, and marketing bulk drugs and formulations. Under the DRL umbrella, there is also a sophisticated life sciences contract R&D unit, called Aurigene Discovery Technologies.

Soon after DRL began its corporate existence as a supplier of bulk "actives" (i.e., pharmaceutical ingredients) to Indian drug manufacturers, it began exporting to other, less regulated markets. With this process, DRL did not have to manufacture in FDA-approved facilities, which demanded costly, time-consuming certification procedures. Therefore, much of DRL's early success came in unregulated markets, in which patents could apply to processes but not products. In such markets, the company could reverse-engineer patented drugs from the developed world and sell them, royalty free, in developing nations such as India and Russia. The founder, Dr. Anji Reddy, gave the company its name but also the foresight to understand that this operating model could not last forever. Realizing that IP regimes around the world would eventually become more harmonized, he began articulating a vision that would transform DRL into a "discovery-led global pharmaceutical company."

In particular, DRL management began to question whether the R&D outsourcing opportunities being exploited in other industries (e.g., software, hardware, electronics) might be profitable in the life sciences, too. After toying with the idea of establishing a new division to offer contract R&D services, in 2001 DRL ultimately decided on setting up a separate company, known as Aurigene Discovery Technologies, with offices located in Bengaluru and Boston. Today, Aurigene is listed on both the New York Stock Exchange and the Bombay Stock Exchange, with significant operations throughout the United States and Europe.

The business model for Aurigene, which officially provides collaborative drug discovery services for lead generation and optimization, focuses on forming partnerships that function on a risk- and reward-sharing basis. At the moment, Aurigene is identifying and building portfolios of product opportunities in several critical health areas, such as metabolic disorders, cardiovascular disease, oncology, and inflammatory conditions.

The idea of contract R&D services in drug discovery certainly was not new in 2001, but most firms with similar business models existed only in the West. Aurigene's onshore-offshore combination made it unique and allowed the company to leverage substantial cost advantages by moving work, if possible, to its Bengaluru offices. The Boston office mostly contained U.S.-based recruits. Despite its small size, the Boston branch served two key functions: it conducted sufficient R&D activity to prove its capabilities and credibility to U.S. clients, and because this U.S. presence bound Aurigene to the U.S. judicial system, it helped address the IP protection concerns of Aurigene's potential clients.

Many customers have taken advantage of Aurigene's R&D offshore outsourcing model. The Debiopharm Group, a global independent biopharmaceutical development company, signed a research agreement with Aurigene to identify and develop compounds for two immuno-oncology targets. Aurigene also recently announced collaborative research agreements with Forest Laboratories Holdings and Merck Serono.[4]

To understand the anatomy of an R&D offshore outsourcing project in the life sciences, let's take a closer look at the terms of Aurigene's agreement with Forest Labs. The two companies entered into a collaboration agreement to discover small-molecule drug candidates for a novel drug that would target obesity and metabolic disorders. Under the terms of the agreement, Aurigene undertook the discovery and optimization of lead compounds, with close participation by Forest Labs' scientists. This work largely took place in Bengaluru. Then all subsequent drug development and commercialization became the responsibility of Forest Labs. In addition, Forest Labs retained full ownership and unencumbered worldwide rights of the compounds developed during the collaboration. However, Forest Labs would pay Aurigene research milestone payments, according to a predefined research plan, and would then pay again when the products of the collaboration, the commercialized compounds, achieved sales milestones. Aurigene thus could potentially receive more than $60 million in development and sales milestone payments if a compound it had helped develop ultimately were successfully commercialized.[5]

Unlike Wipro, DRL's entry into R&D services was premeditated, as well as inspired by the success of the Indian IT services industry (which did not even exist when Wipro began its R&D services activities). But the factors that pushed both firms to pursue these opportunities appear remarkably similar, including the availability of talent at a scale and cost advantages, the realization that not all parts of product development must be performed in one location, and the knowledge that careful management can overcome institutional constraints (e.g., weak IP regime). The examples of Wipro and Aurigene show that R&D outsourcing in the life sciences and engineering domains goes well beyond simply maintaining legacy IT systems, running back offices, or answering calls. And yet, as should come as no surprise at this point in the book, none of this innovative activity is normally visible to the international end consumers who ultimately use the innovations these companies create.

From Services to Innovation: A Thorny Path

Wipro is not alone among India's major IT firms to earn significant R&D outsourcing revenues; others include HCL Technologies, Tata Consulting Services, and Infosys. In the life sciences, too, DRL is not alone. A number of other companies, including Biocon and Nicholas Piramal, offer R&D services; there is also a booming clinical trials segment in India. These several examples, however, do not mean that moving from outsourcing services to offering innovation services has been easy for these companies, or that firms that attempt a similar transition in the future will find the change easy. To understand why, we consider some significant differences between the two business models in which Wipro simultaneously engages: PES and IT services.

To begin with, R&D service engagements have longer lives. For example, whereas Wipro's R&D relationships last between three and eighteen years, its IT service engagements average only one to five years. This difference may reflect the type of relationships that characterize the two forms of service: when it provides R&D services, Wipro jointly engineers a solution with its client, which makes Wipro, in effect, an extended arm of the client's engineering team. Therefore, the partnership norm implies designer-to-designer interactions, rather than a buyer-supplier relationship. In contrast, IT service clients buy the services Wipro provides. This relationship offers more freedom in relation to the client, because the cost, overhead, and price constraints that Wipro confronts are specific and entail fewer dimensions. The collaborative engineering demanded by the R&D services business instead requires Wipro to submit work that the client deems acceptable, according to its stringent global standards and processes. Therefore, what Wipro develops and what it needs to comply with to satisfy the client are much more closely integrated.

Furthermore, the decision makers on the client side differ for R&D and IT services. When it comes to R&D services, the client's chief technology officer, vice president of engineering, or director of engineering usually makes the key choices. For IT services, though, it is typically the chief information officer. For Wipro, this distinction means that the company must meet unique expectations of deliverables and outcomes, which tend to differ across these diverse types of managers.

Major technological differences exist as well. A large portion of what Wipro provides for clients in R&D services takes place in embedded systems, owned by and held at client locations, creating further task interdependence between Wipro's engineers and the client's engineers. For IT services, Wipro can use standardized hardware and software environments instead. For example, if Wipro engineers were developing an application for Linux, they would not need to know a lot about how that application would be implemented in low-level languages. The R&D services designer, in contrast, needs to know just how the application works and which implementations take place in the low-level languages.

Finally, but perhaps most important, hiring and training are very different in the two businesses. As we noted previously, R&D outsourcing to companies like Wipro and Aurigene is as likely to be motivated by the dearth of human resources in the West as by the sheer cost savings (which are considerable). In India, about 650,000 postgraduates and 1,500 PhD students qualify annually in biosciences and engineering, and approximately 150,000 MSc students graduate in chemistry alone.[6] The availability of this talent is the very backbone of the R&D outsourcing sector. However, the screening criteria for selecting talent from this pool are far more stringent for R&D outsourcing work than for IT services.

For example, for PES, Wipro recruits employees with computer science and electrical and communication engineering backgrounds. A new hire with an electrical engineering background will work on board development, system-on-a-chip development, and component characterization, whereas the employees with a computer science and engineering background will write the embedded and protocol software using Java and middleware. In contrast, in the IT services business, Wipro accepts and hires people with mechanical engineering backgrounds as well, because, as Wipro's chief technology officer I. Vijaya Kumar explained, "the scale of hiring is not that high, so I don't have to go and compete to hire from civil engineering and mechanical engineering departments with twenty other companies. We could actually take a more selective approach and consciously build relationships with academic institutions. We have students come and work on projects for us. We also do some hiring occasionally in specialized areas like microelectronics."

The real competition in hiring talent comes from the captive R&D units we encountered in chapter 2 and from other Indian subsidiaries of MNCs, such as SGI, STMicroelectronics, Cadence Design Systems, and Motorola. It is not always easy to compete with, for example, Motorola or AstraZeneca for talent, for multiple reasons. According to Kumar, one of their appeals is that "people can be more specialized within the captive units. Their entire identity is built up around one simple product line. We need much higher levels of flexibility and adaptability to multiple technologies compared to what you could get in an in-house product development unit. Thus, the tolerance to variations in what they would work on has to be higher if they want to work with us."

Although the success that companies such as Wipro enjoy in R&D services bodes well for the ever-increasing sophistication of R&D work in India, the nascent nature of these enterprises must be recognized, as Kumar acknowledged: "Only very recently have we begun to develop a vibrant local (i.e., Indian) market. Perhaps this will shape our understanding of product management and product design. But we clearly have some way to go." In the R&D outsourcing business, product management remains in the hands of the client. High-level designs might be done in India, but the genesis of the idea still comes from the West. And that flow is the very definition of R&D outsourcing—innovation on demand.

Perhaps a more interesting question is this: what is next for companies like Wipro and DRL? What prevents them from becoming full-fledged product companies themselves, with their own brands and R&D competencies? In principle, Wipro already has the end-to-end technical capabilities to become a potential competitor to its clients, at least in some domains. For some product lines, according to Vijaya Kumar, Wipro can go all the way from "ASICs (application specific integrated circuit) to applications."

Yet clients do not seem overly concerned, perhaps because many of them already maintain their own R&D captive units in India. Conceivably, innovative work that is part of the client's core—that is, an area in which the client has a competitive advantage—stays within these captive units. The portions that make their way to Wipro thus might represent the technically sophisticated work that is not necessarily a source of competitive advantage to these clients. Research shows, however, that unless explicit steps are taken to preserve knowledge about outsourced competencies, they will eventually be lost—a use-it-or-lose-it rule applies. Maintaining some levels of in-house activity even for those processes that have been outsourced is often found to be helpful in avoiding this problem.[7]

Several organizational features of successful Indian IT services companies also make it more difficult for these companies to make the transition to branded products. Kumar talked about the problem of corporate culture in this approach: "If you thought about the depth-versus-breadth trade-off, in India the corporate culture still is to have as wide a variety of skills as a form of insurance against future conditions. Making the commitment and investment to build deep skills rather than broad skills is still a cultural change waiting to happen." Nor would companies like Wipro undeniably benefit from launching their own branded products; a branded product development company is not necessarily better than a services company. Branding is risky, requires huge investments, and has uncertain and delayed paybacks. For every popular brand like Google, Apple, and Intel, thousands more have disappeared into obscurity and failure.

Finally, a company like Wipro may be forced to pay a strategic penalty if it were to become an end-to-end player on its own, rather than for its customers, because it would be likely to lose guaranteed revenue from several clients if it started to compete with them. Perhaps this is why Wipro and similar companies seem content to allow their clients to launch

Is Being a Product Company Necessarily Better?

Even successful, globally branded product companies in the world of information technology do not necessarily have an advantage over firms like Wipro. Using data from Google Finance, we found that in December 2010, Infosys and Wipro achieved trailing twelve-month gross margins of 42 percent and 32 percent, respectively.[8] In the same period, Apple's gross margin was 39 percent, and Dell's was 17 percent. Furthermore, it is also doubtful whether the capital markets would appreciate a change in business models by companies like Wipro and Infosys, because the markets already give these companies high marks for their current approach. In June 2010, Infosys and Wipro obtained forward-looking price-to-earnings ratios of twenty-three and twenty-five, respectively; Apple and Google had price-to-earnings ratios of fourteen and sixteen; and Microsoft, IBM, and Intel hovered around ten (all these companies are listed on the New York Stock Exchange). It would be difficult for any CEO at a successful company like Wipro or Infosys to argue with these verdicts from the capital markets.

products, brand them, and sell them end-to-end, without ever showing their own corporate face to the market.

Recommendations

Both the technical expertise and innovations required by Indian firms providing R&D services on demand are substantial. In many cases, everything except the final branding and distribution for a product may take place in India. Yet much of this innovative capacity remains shielded from the world's gaze, in part by design. The plain truth is that even when the technical skills are available in India, it may not make business sense for many firms to invest in creating Indian Googles, iPods, and Viagras. What does this imply for managers and policy makers?

- MNCs seeking advantage through new product development and innovation should take the following approaches:

  - MNCs should recognize that using India as a platform for parts of their innovation processes can make eminent sense. But these corporations must choose carefully to keep within their own Indian captive units those parts that are critical for competitive advantage.

  - MNCs need to recognize that future developments in the technology outsourced will be owned by the third-party Indian outsourcing firm. Multinationals will lose their knowledge advantage over time— unless they explicitly invest in preserving this knowledge.

- Western policy makers should be cognizant of several aspects of outsourcing innovation to countries like India:

  - Facing cost and competitive pressures, many Indian outsourcing companies are moving into higher-value-added R&D services.

- Even technology intensive MNCs increasingly see outsourcing parts of R&D and new product development projects to Indian outsourcing firms as best practice.

- As Indian firms gain experience with such projects, they acquire new capabilities that their MNC clients may end up losing.

- Indian outsourcing firms wishing to migrate into higher-value-added R&D services, which is still an emerging business line, have to transform themselves:

  - They must move from establishing relationships with the chief information officer to the chief technology officer.

  - Instead of managing costs and profitability over relatively short-term contracts, the Indian firms must move to longer-term contracts with associated higher risks.

  - Rather than hiring and training large numbers of people for flexibility so that they can be moved easily between assignments and projects, Indian outsourcing firms need to locate highly specialized people with quality and depth of expertise where India has limited supply.

- Indian outsourcing companies in R&D services may not necessarily be the ones that pioneer branded product development in India, for several reasons:

  - Their culture and mind-set may favor breadth over depth in their work bench.

- The margins are higher in their existing contract research operations than they would be with branded products.

- There is a danger that their existing clients may view them as competitors.

4 Process Innovation
An Injection
of Intelligence

PROCESS INNOVATIONS, or improvements in the *way* something is produced (in contrast with product innovations, which pertain to *what* is being produced), are typically invisible to end consumers. India has a long history of process innovations in sectors such as pharmaceuticals, in which the absence of product patents forced (or, we might say, seduced) Indian companies to focus their R&D efforts on process reengineering. However, in several new domains today, Indian process innovations are coming to the fore and might grow to become visible—if not to end consumers, certainly to global customers. Surprisingly, these process innovations tend to originate in the less glamorous parts of the economy—generic drugs, call centers, knowledge process outsourcing, and even metal forging.

Although improving the way an existing product or service is delivered does not typically bestow the same global visibility on a company as does building something utterly new, the examples in this chapter demonstrate just how powerful these innovations can be. Some of the process innovations in companies such as 24/7 Customer, Bharat Forge, and DenuoSource also exemplify an unusual property: they *stimulate* the creation of new products and services for global B2B markets. That is, they are reversing the conventional picture of innovation. In this conventional, product-centric perspective, a product innovation generates a discontinuous jump in performance and defines a new trajectory; this new product then stimulates a series of process innovations that refine it, and the process is then followed by the next big product innovation, and so on.

In contrast, process innovations can provide foundations on which world-class and globally visible Indian companies can emerge. In the world of services, process innovations can even become a platform for launching novel product innovations and global brands. India may have an advantage in this kind of process innovation because of what we call the *injection of intelligence* effect. The idea behind the concept is simple: companies in some of the less glamorous industries in India today employ people of a much higher caliber than do their counterparts in similar industries in the West. These industries in India can attract superior (some would even say overqualified) talent relative to their Western counterparts, mostly because of the different portfolios of career options across countries. Consequently, an injection of intelligence gives new life to industries that the West has largely written off as dead ends for innovation, resulting in process innovations and sometimes even the development of new products.

World-Class Products from Process Innovations

Consider the history of the pharmaceutical sector in India. Between 1970 and 2005, in a bid to make medicines more broadly available to the impoverished population, Indian laws allowed patents on manufacturing processes but not products. As a result, there arose an entire generics industry that reverse-engineered multinational pharmaceutical companies' patent-protected drugs and then manufactured them using slightly modified processes. The laser-like focus on generics since 1970 has led Indian companies to develop their unique formulations into an extremely lucrative and fast-growing generics business. Companies such as Cipla, Dr. Reddy's Laboratories, Glenmark Generics, Lupin Pharmaceuticals, Ranbaxy Laboratories Limited, Sun Pharmaceutical Industries, and Wockhardt Limited not only dominated the Indian market but also built a substantial export business in off-patent drugs. These were sold initially to the developing world, but, more recently, to the developed world. By 2005, a dozen Indian companies were selling generics in the United States, and they accounted for about 20 percent of the world's $48 billion generic industry.[1]

In contrast with the rest of the world, especially the developed world, where the best brains in the pharmaceutical sector are directed into the discovery of new molecules, the best brains in India have been diverted to reverse-engineering and generics. The result? India had become a hot spot for the development and manufacturing of generics. In its desire to export more to the Western world, India has built the largest number of U.S. FDA-approved plants outside the United States. Indian companies have therefore developed a deep competence in meeting the regulatory requirements of the United States and the European Union.

In 2005, when India agreed to comply with the international patent regime, multinational pharmaceutical companies were anxious to tap into these Indian "invisible innovation" capabilities—whether by setting up captive R&D centers in India (e.g., AstraZeneca) or by subcontracting R&D processes, such as early-stage discovery activities, to Indian companies (e.g., Aurigene Discovery Technologies by Dr. Reddy's Laboratories). Both strategies targeted savings on drug discovery and development costs (as much as 50 percent), but perhaps even more important, they allowed Indian companies to leverage their unique formulations of foreign patented drugs for the Indian market. Because branded generics represent a significant business for most of the major global pharmaceutical companies, many of these companies picked up the Indian formulations and applied their global marketing expertise and worldwide distribution muscle to the drugs. Recently, several alliances have combined Indian generics companies with Western pharmaceutical firms to market these Indian generics all over the world.

Consider the initiatives of Pfizer, the second-largest pharmaceutical company in the world (after Johnson & Johnson), with global revenues in excess of $50 billion. In 2009, Pfizer bought the rights for forty-nine generic drugs in pill form and another twelve in injectable form from the Hyderabad-based Aurobindo Pharma to sell in the United States and Europe. This deal represented the first time that Pfizer agreed to sell medicines discovered by other companies. In the same year, Pfizer entered a license agreement with another Indian firm, Claris Lifesciences, to market fifteen off-patent injectable drugs. Then a collaboration to commercialize products manufactured by Strides, including off-patent sterile injectable and oral products, for markets in the European Union, Canada, Australia, New Zealand, Japan, and Korea added another forty-five generic products to Pfizer's portfolio. Continuing this strategy, Pfizer paid $200 million in 2010 (with the option to pay another $150 million if regulatory hurdles were overcome) for the right to market biosimilar insulin formulations created by Biocon, another leading Indian biotechnology company. Pfizer obtained exclusive access to several Biocon biosimilars, including Biocon's recombinant human insulin; glargine, a generic of Sanofi-Aventis's long-acting Lantus; aspart, a generic of Novo Nordisk's fast-acting Novo-Log; and a generic of Eli Lilly's fast-acting Lispro. Again, most of these examples represent invisible innovation as patients in the developed world will probably never know that these Pfizer-branded offerings are actually generics developed in India. Therefore, what began as process innovations in the generics business by Indian firms has morphed into globally competitive products, branded by other companies.

To go to an entirely different industry, consider Bharat Forge, which manufactures various metal forged and machined components for the automotive and other sectors.[2] It experienced dramatic success in the form of export-driven domestic growth when it changed its workforce from muscle power to brain power. Historically, the combination of available cheap manual labor and high capital costs led Indian companies to make an archaic trade-off: instead of investing in technologically sophisticated production equipment, they employed a massive blue-collar workforce in labor-intensive manual production processes. In this action, Bharat Forge was no exception; most of its hammer-shop operations for making forgings were manual. However, CEO Baba Kalyani soon came to realize the impossibility of consistently making world-class products using manual processes. He correctly identified the core competencies in which Bharat Forge would need to invest to become a player on the world stage: speed to market, high quality, low cost, volume, production flexibility, and a distinctly customer-focused orientation. He also realized that these competencies were not possible without a highly trained, motivated, and productive workforce. To realize this vision, Bharat Forge would need to invest considerably in technology, in the hope of gaining a future advantage.

In the late 1980s, Bharat Forge therefore acquired several new, state-of-the-art, fully automated press lines for manufacturing forgings, even though the existing manual workforce in the hammer shop did not know how to operate them. The company placed these new machines in a brand-new workshop, run by freshly recruited, young white-collar employees with science-based degrees. Unlike the old forging shop, where workers possessed narrow specializations (e.g., machinist, grinder, fitter), this new workforce would be multiskilled and capable of performing several jobs, at very high levels of productivity. The older manual employees could retire early, and many chose to do so. The remaining employees received extensive training to upgrade their skills.

The impact of this transformation was dramatic. The company moved from an 85 percent blue-collar workforce in 1989 to an 85 percent white-collar workforce by 2000, including more than seven hundred engineers. Because the company owned so many engineering resources, compared with global competitors, it could improve quality and increase speed, even as it lowered costs. Kalyani described these advantages: "We brought in one simple strategy of speed to market to overcome challenges. We created a process to do things in a third of the time a European or American company took to do similar tasks, using technology. ArvinMeritor [a tier-one automotive supplier] visited our plant and found us producing a part for their automobiles in just three weeks from scratch. They were blown away. We used speed to market to develop the confidence. We did the same thing with Caterpillar. Low cost, high technologies, and speed of delivery have all helped us to be accepted in the Western markets."

What Kalyani does not emphasize, though, is that it was not merely the technology, but also the use of highly qualified talent (perhaps even overqualified talent, by Western standards) that enabled Bharat Forge to gain a technological edge over its Western rivals.

As the examples of Pfizer and Bharat Forge show, the availability of talent at a reasonable cost often pushes Indian companies to assign what the developed world would consider overqualified people to relatively mundane processes. This injection of intelligence can then lead to process innovations that provide the basis for globally competitive processes and products. To take another case in point, consider that it is perhaps only in India that millions of young people aspire to work in a call center!

From Taking Calls to Reading Minds

The customer-contact business has evolved significantly during the past few decades, especially because of offshoring and the growth of the Internet.[3] But in some fundamental ways, the business has not really changed. Contact with customers can now take place through multiple media channels, including call centers halfway around the world, yet the basic business is still about responding to customer queries or contacting large numbers of customers in the hope of selling to at least a few. By injecting intelligence into their call centers, though, some companies are changing such practices.

A Silicon Valley start-up, 24/7 Customer handles upward of ten million customer contacts each month for global clients, including retailers, mobile phone service providers, financial services companies, and firms in the hospitality industry. Beginning in 2000, when, as a hundred-seat call center, the company started providing standard services from Bengaluru, 24/7 Customer has expanded to include seven thousand seats. This remarkable growth followed mostly from a standard outsourcing growth model: add seats, add revenue. This simple, highly profitable model is perfect for the outsourcing industry, in which revenues are typically linked to the number of customer interactions. Thus far, 24/7 Customer's story sounds just like that of many other IT and business process outsourcing start-ups in India. In particular, a skilled labor force with high proficiency in spoken English (at less than half the domestic U.S.-European labor cost) helped Indian firms that outsource business processes reach a 30 percent average growth rate from 2004 to 2008. This model offered profitability, but was also accompanied by high staff churn, because growing companies in every major city in India fought for talent.

Around 2005, 24/7 Customer's management recognized a shift in its competitive arena, as V. Bharathwaj ("Bharath"), 24/7 Customer's chief marketing officer, explained: "It was becoming evident that outsourcing providers were splitting into two types . . . generalists, who provided basic service levels, or specialists, providing premium services. The generalists competed primarily on cost and scale, and the advantage was with the large, global suppliers like Convergys and IBM. 24/7 Customer couldn't match their size and knew we would have to compete differently . . . While we couldn't compete on cost, we could compete on innovation."

Competition can be a spur to innovation, even in an allegedly low-tech sector such as the call center business. But having the talent in place to deliver it is what makes 24/7 Customer such an unusual company in the industry.

The management team sought a specialist area in which it could add value for clients. To start, 24/7 Customer looked internally at its capacities and realized that the data mining work it was already handling for clients offered a value-added opportunity. The company developed tools that collated data about the past behavior of customers and mined this information for patterns and other clues that might indicate customers' intentions. For example, the company found that many people who visited a commercial Web site intending to buy something eventually gave up, usually because they were confused—by the product descriptions, navigation, or checkout procedures. So 24/7 Customer's iLabs division developed SalesNext, a proprietary business intelligence tool set, for clients such as Adobe Systems and CapitalOne Financial Group. With these tools, contact center agents intervene at crucial points in transactions and help convert more than 15 percent of Web site visitors into buyers, compared with base rate data that shows that on average, only 1 to 3 percent of all Web site visits ended in transactions. P. V. Kannan, CEO of 24/7 Customer, succinctly summarized the result: "Clients get buyers, not browsers."

The general approach adopted by 24/7 Customer's predictive-modeling products works like this: using behavior mapping models, the company estimates a customer's income and sensitivity to a price point. By analyzing a recorded selection of the customer's voice, the tool can gauge his or her emotional state and then combine this information with the customer's history with the company and frequency of contact. Web site visitors are then classified as hot or cold leads. For example, the firm can now predict that a man visiting a Web site on a Wednesday afternoon between 3 p.m. and 5 p.m., through a cable connection from San Jose, with a U.S. postal code ending in 42, is more likely to buy Product X than is a woman visiting on a Thursday morning between 10 a.m. and 11 a.m., through a dial-up connection from San Antonio, with a U.S. postal code ending in 18, when both of them are browsing the jewelry section for at least five minutes. Contact center agents therefore make personalized contact with the most promising leads through Web chats, using this form of interactivity to move the visitor from browsing to purchasing.

The predictive-modeling product enables a knowledge-driven intervention in real time (through chat or voice), which results in high-quality assistance to the right prospect, at the right time, with the right offer, with the right contact center specialist agent. The company applies this product to all its channels, whether they be Web or voice or e-mail.

The same logic applies to the service side, where 24/7 Customer's ServiceNext analytical tools can predict when customer service intervention is needed and, if so, can then help formulate an individualized response. The technology is proprietary, and patents in the U.S. patent regime are pending.

The underlying goal behind this innovative approach is to reduce redundant interactions and thus minimize call center contacts, customer frustration, and, ultimately, costs. For example, banking, insurance, and telecommunications sectors typically entail high customer engagement levels, which lead to high operational costs and many potential moments in which customer satisfaction can be ruined. Therefore, iLabs came up with a process to mine customer engagement data and current market events and then combined these with product life-cycle data and regional demographics. Such business intelligence offers a good prediction of the questions and responses an individual customer might have and thereby matches the best contact channel (e-mail, chat, voice) or agent to the customer, all in real time. The system then tracks customers' behavior and feeds it back into the tool set, to allow for changing model variables and dynamic refinements to the whole process. Thus, the "voice of the customer" rings out clearly. iLabs claimed 80 percent accuracy for its predictive thresholds.

Kannan suggested thinking of this system as "an ecosystem comprising the Web site's business managers, who may be in the USA, the contact center agents, who may be sitting in Mexico or anywhere else in the world, the mathematicians and statisticians predicting the interaction, who may be sitting in India or Eastern Europe and the global operations center . . . They all collaborate to provide a unique dynamic experience for every visitor who comes to the client Web site or contact center."

By 2009, about twelve clients in retail, technology, financial services, and telecommunications space had joined this ecosystem by subscribing to the predictive analytical services at iLabs. The clients constituted about one-third of 24/7 Customer's entire customer base. "We are improving conversions, improving customer satisfaction, and increasing customer stickiness while reducing costs," Bharath noted. "Our clients are seeing results, and since these are proprietary, intellectual-property-driven services, these are typically high-profit, high-value deals for us." Live video might be the next extension of Web site interventions, he said. "We haven't added a video component yet; consumers are just warming up to text chatting . . . This is still leading edge."

By its very nature, the purpose of Web commerce is to minimize human contact. As voice-based customer care becomes relatively more expensive, could this technology actually eliminate the need for human touch? Staff typically accounts for about 70 percent of the cost of running a call center, so could economic forces be pushing toward the elimination of call centers? Bharath disagreed. Even if a firm deploys all the intelligent customer-service products possible, he maintained that complete automation is not achievable or even desirable: "Commerce will never be 100 percent human-interface free. Humans are hardwired to connect. That is an incredible marketing opportunity! By carefully understanding and respecting this need, you can build lifetime loyalty and goodwill for your brand, cheaper and more efficiently than ever before. We are at the technological forefront of this ability, and innovations will continue to be uncovered—by humans!"

Turning Art into Science

Let us consider another example from an industry that is perceived to have higher levels of technical sophistication than that associated with typical call center work.[4] Despite these technical differences, the path to product development for DenuoSource—a small, private analytics firm with operations in North America, Europe, and Asia-Pacific—is similar to that of 24/7 Customer. Since DenuoSource's inception in 2006, the client base has multiplied, profits have increased at a steady rate, and the company has grown from a mere vision of two classmates at the Kellogg School of Management—namely, Rahul Chowdhury and Amrit Kriplani—to a team of more than 150 professionals.

A few years ago, DenuoSource landed a unique opportunity with an existing customer, a large *Fortune* 500 retailer, that faced the common dilemma of determining the appropriate markets in which to open new stores. Location analysis and sales forecasting traditionally have been considered an art, carried out by real estate or finance departments, with inputs provided by analytics companies such as DenuoSource. But DenuoSource saw an opportunity to do more than just provide inputs to the decision. It could create an algorithmic approach to solving the problem, and the approach itself could be sold as a product.

DenuoSource therefore developed its Location Analyzer product to turn the art of location analysis and sales forecasting into a science. This tool helps businesses such as retail chains, malls, fast-food restaurants, or real estate developers decide whether it would be beneficial to open a new store and, if so, where the businesses should place the store to increase their chances of success. Geographical sales, store characteristics, and demographics get plugged into the software, which returns a scorecard of the different locations and their relative strengths. The Location Analyzer also helps businesses determine whether remodeling or relocating existing stores would be worth the time, effort, and expense. Such information is critical; research shows that retailers lose millions on remodeling efforts, considering that remodeling can cost $10 million to $15 million per store. With its unique approach to integrating GIS (geographical information system) data with store and demographic data, DenuoSource provides valuable insight for decisions about a given site.

Turning Services into Products

Despite their different industries and products, the 24/7 Customer and DenuoSource stories have several features in common. In both cases, the firms' primary business was to provide outsourced services to clients. Both companies found innovative ways to meet the needs of their clients, with the understanding that this improvement in delivering services could also be customized into actual products. That is, 24/7 Customer and DenuoSource created novel IP and new product lines.

Remarkably, 24/7 Customer, a call center company, was one of the first firms to realize the opportunity in, and develop the capabilities for, the delivery of extremely high-end predictive analytics capabilities. The fifty staff members who work on predictive modeling solutions in the company's iLab unit include mathematicians, statisticians, process experts, and analysts. They represent a mix of PhDs and MBAs, and nearly all have undergraduate degrees in mathematics, physics, computer science, or engineering. And they happily file patents for their innovations! None of these descriptors is typical of a call center company in the West. As this example shows, the services outsourcing sector in India is particularly receptive to an injection of intelligence into fairly standardized, commodity-like services, because of the higher margins and employee qualifications that characterize such Indian companies in comparison with their Western counterparts. It is not unusual to find people with high-level degrees taking calls, and the CEOs of such companies tend to be extremely tech-savvy (as is 24/7 Customer's Kannan, undoubtedly; his previous venture was a software company that he sold to Siebel Systems). This picture creates a stark contrast with the high school dropout stereotype of call center employees in the West.

Although DenuoSource is an intrinsically higher-skill business model (analytics), the amount of initiative an analytics services provider can take to serve its clients varies. The company's self-conscious positioning at the higher end of this spectrum is clearly evident in its communications to potential hires. Senior managers call the company an "intellectual playground, where analytical sciences lead to profitability." The routine and monotonous work associated with larger analytic outfits cannot fit this description, but the variety of Denuo-Source's clients and their complex, distinct business problems help retain and motivate its human resources. The company believes that this variety leads to reduced labor turnover and attrition, which can also ultimately mean lower costs.

Recommendations

A unique feature of the Indian economy is the ability of certain sectors to attract talent with qualifications vastly superior to the qualifications of those employed in the same sectors in Western countries. Compared with the Indian workforce, Western employees with comparable qualifications and talent are much less likely to work on generics, metal forgings, call centers, or simple analytics jobs. This unique situation has an interesting second-order effect: innovation flourishes in what were previously considered mature or low-tech settings. Some process innovations underlie globally competitive companies; others have the potential to be customized into products for the world, in both business and end consumer markets. The injection of intelligence thus gives India an advantage at yet another form of invisible innovation. What does this imply for policy makers and managers?

- MNCs should consider the following actions:

  - When outsourcing to Indian third parties or their own captives in India, MNCs should demand innovation rather than restrict themselves to being satisfied by cost savings.

  - MNCs should scan the Indian industry in sectors that are attractive in India but that are given up for dead in the West. In these sectors, there may be opportunities to tap into innovation developed in India. Marrying these Indian innovations with the global marketing and distribution networks of MNCs could be a successful undertaking.

- Western policy makers should realize that sectors that are considered old and traditional may still have process innovation potential that may ultimately spawn new products.

- Indian companies, especially outsourcing firms, should intensely examine how to exploit the injection-of-intelligence phenomenon for process innovations that can help develop new capabilities and products.

5 Management Innovation
The Global
Delivery Model

INNOVATIONS THAT MAKE evident changes in people's daily lives are obvious to end consumers. Management innovations—the implementation of new management practices, processes, or structures that significantly alter how work is performed—instead are neither evident nor obvious. Instead, they are typically invisible to end customers. Few of these innovations have the spotlight cast upon them unless their champions are enthused enough to write widely about them. Julian Birkinshaw and Gary Hamel, our colleagues at London Business School, have pointed out some of these management innovations: the development of the modern corporate R&D lab and widespread application of Six Sigma quality assurance practices by General Electric (GE), DuPont's invention of capital budgeting tools, the adoption of the M-form organizational structure by General Motors, and Toyota's success in harnessing the problem-solving skills of first-level employees.[1] The global services delivery model (abbreviated to global delivery model) belongs in this category, too.[2] It may be India's most invisible innovation, though its consequences, ranging from phone calls from people with strange accents to fears of the movement of white-collar jobs, have, of course, been highly visible to people in the West.

Invented, or perhaps simultaneously developed, in the late 1990s by many Indian IT companies, this model allows for a key transformation: tightly integrated tasks formerly performed by workers in one location working for a single company now take on a distributed format, such that different parts of the work are executed in different geographies and by different organizations. The advantages are obvious, including the ability to (1) execute the work where the best expertise exists at the lowest possible costs, (2) take advantage of time zone differences for round-the-clock efforts, and (3) achieve some level of risk diversification by building redundancy across locations. The potential challenges are equally obvious: how to get people to work effectively across barriers erected by organizations, nations, cultures, and time zones.

The global delivery model was initially created to deliver IT and back-office services to Western clients, but it has become fundamental to other kinds of invisible innovations as well. For example, the R&D captive units, R&D services outsourcing companies, or even the process-to-product innovations we have discussed thus far probably could not have succeeded in the absence of a global delivery model. Simply put, its role is critical to any discussion of how innovation created in India affects the rest of the world. Beyond integrating the parallel development efforts by innovators, engineers, and scientists worldwide, this model offers to Indian innovators some insight on Western customers.

The Death of Distance? Not Quite, but . . .

Students and seminar audiences often ask us, somewhat skeptically, just how widely applicable the global delivery model really is. By now everybody has probably heard the argument: "I still have to get my haircut/eat my meals/have my tailoring done right here. Try offshoring that!" Our usual rejoinder is, "Fine, but someone can book your appointment/reserve your table/do the actual stitching anywhere in the world." The attractions of wage arbitrage and specialization have always pushed people to find ways to divide tasks across people and organizations. The global delivery model offers a systematic method for doing so.

Intuitively, this process should work well for fairly routine, mundane, standardized tasks (e.g., booking flights and making restaurant reservations). Can it work just as well for high-value-added knowledge work or creative work such as movie making, R&D, or analytics? This may in fact be asking the wrong question. The key insight from our research into the global delivery model is that the ability to execute a task remotely has little relation to whether the work itself is simple and standardized. Rather, it depends on whether the *links* across the subtasks can be managed across distances. If work

Almost Telepathy . . .

In two research studies conducted with Kannan Srikanth of the Indian School of Business, one of us examined what makes global delivery difficult but still feasible. Across 126 business processes, we measured the level of standardization and documentation of processes (before offshoring) as well as the level of standardization of the links between this process and others. Only the latter measure is statistically associated with how effectively the process can be managed offshore. In principle, as long as the links are clear and standard, even the most unstructured and creative tasks can be moved to remote locations.

Our second study found something even more remarkable. Even when the links between processes are not standardized, organizations can often find ways to make them work in separate locations as if the processes were being executed in adjacent rooms![3] We studied about sixty colocated and distributed projects and came to the surprising conclusion

---

can be divided into chunks that can be executed more or less independently, whether the chunks themselves involve creative or standardized work matter less. It seems like a simple idea, but it took us about two years to confirm it with data.[4]

And for the evidence that work that is more creative can be offshored, consider Tata Elxsi. This division of the Tata Group set up a unit in Santa Monica and hired Academy Award–winning special effects artist Joel Hynek to get a slice of the Hollywood action.[5] The work will be divided between

that some companies had figured out ways to let engineers in different locations coordinate their iterative programming and bug-fixing activities—without the need for extensive communication.

The engineers drew on their common ground—that is, the knowledge they shared and knew was shared—to anticipate how other engineers would respond to programming problems. By knowing what their fellow engineers knew, they could coordinate actions without extensive face-to-face communication. This stock of shared knowledge came from the engineers' common training in the company, as well as the use of workflow software that made the programming context of each site visible to other sites. Even when they were left with only poor substitutes for face-to-face interaction (e.g., webcams, telephones, e-mail), these engineers managed to achieve "cognitive collocation" and thus success. To a naive observer, the extent to which these engineers coordinated without the need for direct communication may seem almost like telepathy!

the Hollywood branch and Tata Elxsi's Mumbai offices, much the same way that Aurigene Discovery Technologies split contract R&D work between its Boston and Bengaluru offices (chapter 3). Having worked on movies like *Spider-Man 3*, Tata Elxsi estimated that about a quarter of the most sophisticated work on a film is kept for its California office, with the remainder being done in India. The effective cost savings to clients could be as much as 40 percent, and as a result, Hollywood is moving from outsourcing basic functions to having

Indian visual effects firms bid for larger and more complete contracts.

Undoubtedly, barriers both natural (e.g., cultural, distance) and manufactured (e.g., tariffs, import duties) impede the forces of global competition.[6] But the kinds of organizational innovations that underlie the global delivery model are steadily reducing these barriers, even for those who rest in the apparent security of creative, nonstandardized jobs. Reducing these barriers even if it does not result in the movement of jobs offshore can affect wages, because jobs become contestable once there is proof of concept that the same work can be done remotely. The global delivery model, applied to widely distinctive sectors (e.g., back-office services, call centers, IT development, legal services, product engineering services, life sciences R&D, animation and film special effects), is furnishing such proof in all areas.

The Anatomy of the Global Delivery Model

Let's take a closer look at how the global delivery model works in the setting in which it originated—business process outsourcing.[7] Assume that a client company, located in either the United States or Europe, decides to offshore particular processes (e.g., IT systems maintenance, stock trading, mortgage processing). The client selects a vendor and a location, such as India or the Philippines, from which the service is to be implemented.

Offshoring begins with an on-site visit (i.e., at the client's current location) by a small team of vendor personnel, usually called the *migration team* or *transition team*, to understand the details of the process. The team's goal is to realize how the process currently operates, including both its internal workings and its connection to surrounding processes.

For example, preparing to move credit card application approval offshore requires the team to comprehend the steps associated with evaluating an application (which can typically be done offshore) and how these steps interact with other processes such as marketing and customer support (which typically remain onshore). The vendor team studies how the process operates, either through observation or by performing the work themselves, under the supervision of client personnel. To support such knowledge transfer activities, the team extensively documents the policies and procedures that dictate how the process should work, as well as how it currently works. In many cases, shockingly, this step by the transition team marks the first time anyone has attempted to document the process!

Next, the vendor team has to determine how it will deal with interdependencies across processes. For example, in a credit card approval, an employee could manage interdependence between two adjacent steps in the process by walking over to the next cubicle to have a short discussion with another employee, then using the information and decisions gained in that interaction to structure the next steps. But offshoring precludes such a simple approach, so the vendor team must decide how to manage this link between employees on different sides of the globe. In principle, it could map out all such possible dependencies and formalize them (e.g., as in an electronic data interchange system). Alternately, the team could decide that this interaction is possible through e-mail, telephone, or other such tools. Failing all these options, the team might determine that this portion of the process has to remain on site.

After its on-site visit and analysis, the vendor team moves to the offshore location, where it forms the core of the team that implements the transition. The vendor team now manages the knowledge transfer to other offshore personnel, and the business process is often performed in parallel in both locations for a while. Over several weeks, the offshore volume ramps up as the on-site volume decreases. During this ramp-up phase, any further bugs get worked out of the offshored process, and both offshore and on-site personnel learn from their experience. Reengineering the process usually takes place only after several months of stable production at maximum volume at the offshore location.

Finally, after the process moves to its new location, the focus shifts to ensuring integrated efforts across locations. Hand-offs, communication, and data transfers all must go smoothly—especially if the process involves a *follow-the-sun strategy*, such that the work moves from one location to another as the working day ends in one location and begins in another.

Setting up and running a global delivery model involves solving knowledge-transfer and coordination problems. For instance, when a software maintenance process moves from London to Bengaluru, the Indian employees must learn not only how to do what the maintenance engineers in London were doing (knowledge transfer) but also how to connect with London employees, whose work is interdependent with software maintenance, such as software users (coordination).

Knowledge transfer is easier if process knowledge is standardized and well documented, rather than left unarticulated, held only in the minds of the employees currently executing the process.[8] Similarly, coordination across processes is easier when the interactions between the process and its surroundings are standardized or otherwise easy to accomplish. When the people performing interconnected steps are collocated, these sorts of interactions tend to be ad hoc and face-to-face, particularly if there are problems. But face-to-face problem solving is not possible—or at least not easy—in the global delivery model. Thus, coordination across a wide geographic distance is easier when the *links* between processes are minimized, standardized, and well documented. Both knowledge-transfer-related and coordination-related challenges can create significant organizational overhead and can absorb up to 15 percent to 25 percent of the gains from wage arbitrage in offshoring.[9]

The Global Delivery Model in the Context of Innovation Work

Not only is the global delivery model a form of invisible (management) innovation, but it also supports other forms of invisible innovation. For instance, both globally segmented innovation (chapter 2) and R&D outsourcing (chapter 3) depend on global delivery principles. However, in these higher-value-added activities, the knowledge transfer problem may not be as salient. The movement offshore of complex, nonstandardized processes, such as asset pricing, equity research, or contract R&D, offers a clear example: concerns about knowledge transfer become moot when the offshoring of services shifts away from a service delivery model and toward a content development model, because the client cares about the outcomes, not the exact replication of processes. Therefore, the core challenge for managing the global delivery model to support innovation work is likely to be the coordination of distributed work. Much that we know about how distributed work is coordinated in the global delivery model when applied to simpler work also applies to more complex innovative work.

There are two generic approaches to managing the challenge of ongoing coordination in the global delivery model: separation and integration. With a separation strategy, the goal is to "black-box," or separate, the processes to minimize the interactions of offshore and on-site locations. In contrast, the integration strategy facilitates these interactions to overcome the constraints of distance.

In turn, an integration strategy features one of two clearly different approaches. The first emphasizes coordination across locations through well-established channels—using administrative positions (e.g., program managers) and IT tools (e.g., e-mail, telephone, videoconferencing). If these prove inadequate, vendors may selectively locate a few employees from their organization at client locations—on the theory that it may be easier to work across distances with your own teammates than with the client's team.

The second approach places less emphasis on building communication and more on tacit coordination—that is, coordination without communication. Such an approach relies on shared decision-making procedures, a shared vocabulary, and the ability to observe work in progress across locations. Such mechanisms help both on-site and offshore employees coordinate with one another in that seemingly telepathic method we mentioned among the engineers, without more extensive communication or expensive videoconferencing and travel demands.[10]

To elaborate on these three approaches—namely, the separation and the two integration methods—consider the R&D captive units of MNCs we discussed in chapter 2 (e.g., GE, Intel, Microsoft). These units use the separation—or black-boxing—principle extensively when they establish each location as a distinctive center of expertise. For example, GE's John F. Welch Technology Centre in Bengaluru constitutes GE's global capability for computational modeling. Partitioning work according to expertise is a commonly used means to divide the work across the globe to exploit specialist local skills. However, it also means that the work can proceed largely independently across locations because of either horizontal or vertical segmentation of R&D.

On the other hand, when these distributed pieces of specialist work typically cannot be completely black-boxed, at least the final results across locations must be integrated. To do so, companies can build formal channels for coordination across locations. These include assigning integrating roles (e.g., program managers), locating some employees physically close to others, or opening direct channels of communication (e.g., telephone, e-mail, videoconferencing) to help bridge distances. Ensuring that people speak the same language augments the efficacy of these channels enormously. When we say "the same language," we do not mean (merely) that all parties involved should speak English. At GE, design engineers from R&D centers around the world work effectively together, despite the differences in their native language. "Language-wise, we all speak the Six Sigma language!" said a senior manager at the GE Bengaluru campus. "So, for example, we say 'CTQs,' which you might not understand, but it is 'critical to quality,' which basically means, 'What are the important deliverables for this project?'"

Alternately, distributed work could be integrated without much need for communication across geographies if a shared understanding can be created instead. Tanjore Balganesh at AstraZeneca's Bengaluru unit thus stressed the importance of labeling and entering data in a commonly understood way and putting it in electronic spaces that make it visible anywhere: "When people share the same understanding about work procedures, data, methods, the underlying science, . . . the need to pick up the phone and ask questions really doesn't arise as often." And thus we return to that image of telepathy.

As any magician can tell you, though, telepathy is not easy. Obstacles to the creation of this telepathic effect include a lack of transparency in decision making across locations, nonuniform work environments (e.g., technologies, software, platforms), an overemphasis on cultural differences and underemphasis on cultural similarities, and overreliance on communication, with no attempt to build a shared understanding.

The soft factors underlying mutual understanding and a worldview shared by on-site and offshore personnel have fairly hard economic consequences, in the sense that they can limit the need for travel and help avoid costly coordination failures. Guillermo Wille, head of GE's Bengaluru campus, summarized these softer issues:

Typically, people don't want to trust their counterparts that are sitting eleven thousand miles away. But if you step back and think about the fact, very few companies have the luxury anymore of having all the technologies sitting in one building, on one site. Most companies have different technology teams sitting in different buildings, maybe different cities. And the behavioral reality is that if people are sitting in different buildings, already they pick up the phone and communicate through the computer. So why would people care about sitting in a building eleven thousand miles away? If you understand that simple fact, and you have the culture of treating your teams either in the next building or eleven thousand miles away in the same way, you have it. And then they communicate as if they were sitting just in different buildings. There is one single caveat to that; that's the time difference . . . What it does is it generates issues in work-life balance. That's the only real problem. And you have to compensate for that. And if you understand how to compensate for that, you can manage to really work globally.

But what about managing the flow of physical material? Not every kind of work can be e-mailed. Consider an example from our conversation with Rahul Bedi at Intel:

We have a "hand-carry" process where we can make sure to get physical components from any lab in the world to any other lab in minimal time. I mean, the process has been so fine-tuned to perfection that the engineers even know exactly how much customs we have got to pay in which country . . . You land up in India, you go to the customs guys, custom duties paid right there, walk out. You have a person waiting for you outside the airport [because planes often land at night]. Other guys from our team will carry the item because you are tired, you need to go home—the person will take it from you, he takes it back to the lab, and the team is waiting . . . You see, at the later stages of a project, every hour is crucial because one day of delay could have millions of dollars of implicit cost.

After hearing these comments, we could not help asking Bedi, "So Intel has basically internalized its own FedEx?" His response showed just how much thought is put in to physical transport at Intel: "Well . . . you won't believe the kind of preparation we need to hand-carry stuff. We have a checklist; you can only carry so many clothes because you don't check in your stuff. You have to hand-carry the stuff, and then we have it tested out so that it shouldn't look like something dangerous. Often, you have multiple people converging on a lab with components from around the world, so one guy is going to come in from the East Coast, one from the West Coast, one from Asia . . ." And with that, Intel achieves global delivery in both figurative and literal senses.

Recommendations

The global delivery model is responsible for making the Indian outsourcing industry the success it is today. The model reconceptualizes formerly physically collocated activities by breaking them into subtasks that can be performed virtually anywhere. But it also specifies how the subtasks are ultimately rejoined. The dispersion of work across the world brings both global cost efficiencies and global scale to what were previously locally optimized processes. The principles of the global delivery model have moved beyond the confines of IT services and call centers to higher-value-added and highly innovative work as well. What does this imply for policy makers and managers?

- The Indian management innovation of the global delivery model is leading both to lower costs for MNCs based in high-cost, developed nations and to lower prices for consumers. These advantages arise for several reasons:

  - Indian management innovation of the global delivery model initially brings global scale and efficiencies to services that could be easily offshored.

  - Increasingly, Indian innovation has extended the model to more sophisticated tasks as leading firms are learning how to offshore more complex and creative tasks.

  - It is not simply about investing in high-bandwidth communication channels across locations, but also about leveraging shared knowledge and understanding to minimize the very need for communication.

  The wider applicability of the global delivery model is itself an arena for ongoing innovation—and it is an active one.

- Western policy makers need to realize that advances in the application of the global delivery model have transformed the traditional model:

  - It has moved beyond jobs such as call centers and software development to more sophisticated creative tasks as Indian firms find ways to divide and integrate even sophisticated work across locations.

– Advances in the model have overturned the traditional logic of moving people from the developing world to jobs in the West (immigration) to moving jobs to people through offshoring.

– These advances have also increased the contestability of not just low-skill service jobs but also high-skill innovation-oriented jobs, with resultant downward wage pressures in the West.

6 Visible Innovation
Frugal Engineering

WHILE WE WERE WRITING this book, one of us had the pleasure of attending a screening of the 3-D movie *The Hubble* at the IMAX theater at the Science Museum in London (needless to say, a child was involved). The movie chronicles the twenty-year history of the space telescope and puts viewers in orbit with seven astronauts aboard the space shuttle *Atlantis* on a mission to repair the Hubble. After locating the telescope and docking the ship, pairs of astronauts venture out of *Atlantis* to replace Hubble's malfunctioning parts—while floating in deep space. The astronauts then return safely back to the United States. When the lights came on, the entire movie theater, packed mostly with children, was silent, amazed by this demonstration of technological and innovation prowess.

Seeing the movie naturally prompted us to question whether India could ever reach such levels of innovation. If one thinks about the resources and time spent on the kind of technological innovation that lies behind a Hubble, it seems hard to question the conventional wisdom that innovation is a uniquely Western advantage.[1] But our cinematic experience also put us in a historical frame of mind. Historically, nationalistic competitive impulses have spurred innovation—the Soviet Union's success in sending manned missions to space prompted President John F. Kennedy to challenge creative minds in NASA (National Aeronautics and Space Administration) and the rest of the United States to put a man on the moon within a decade. The demonstration effect on the confidence and competence of a nation should not be underestimated, quite independent of the flow of knowledge and expertise from R&D in the defense and military establishment to the commercial sector. In a similar way, high-profile, visible innovations—quite independent of their commercial viability—could be important means for emerging countries to demonstrate, both to themselves and to others, that they have arrived on the global stage. Thus, for companies from emerging markets, the development of innovative products to sell to the world, especially to end consumers, could mean greater corporate reputation and brand equity.

Ambitious Indian companies realize this point. Although it is already one of the five largest manufacturers of tractors in the world, Mahindra & Mahindra is also pursuing a global position in the sport utility vehicle (SUV) segment. Farmers in the United States might value the Mahindra tractor, but the masses of consumers who buy other vehicles remained unfamiliar with the name. To reach these masses, Vice Chairman Anand Mahindra is convinced that innovative product extension is the key: "SUVs will be what gets us known as a global brand."[2] Mahindra & Mahindra's product, the Scorpio, was launched in 2002 and is sold across many countries in the world. Similarly, developing its innovative Nano car brought Tata Motors far more global awareness than did any of the firm's previous achievements in its seventy-year history. With this innovation, Tata gained sixth place on *BusinessWeek*'s list of the world's fifty most innovative companies, jumping "onto our list for the first time, fueled by its paradigm-busting $2,500 'Nano' car for the masses."[3]

India and Indian companies want to prove themselves. But the West, in the form of thousands of innovative products, ranging from the Hubble telescope to Apple's iPad, maintains a strong lead in the visible innovation race. Perhaps this lead is insurmountable for Indian firms (or, for that matter, Chinese) to overcome. As might be expected, though, the answer is more nuanced. For certain kinds of innovations, particularly those closely linked to basic science, the lead of the West is strong. On the other hand, certain other kinds of innovation are more naturally germinated in contexts like India's. In this chapter, we compare visible innovations originating in the West with examples of visible innovation that increasingly originate in India.

Innovations in the West and in India

Much like the rest of NASA's space program, the Hubble telescope indicates that the United States is unmatched in its innovation capabilities, especially when the focus is on exploring the frontiers of science. The majority of Nobel Prize winners in the sciences perform their research at U.S. universities, often funded by university or government grants that encourage curiosity, knowledge building, and the country's long-term competitive advantage. Over time, some of this new knowledge ultimately results in breakthrough products and services. And this long-standing tradition means that in the short term, countries like India and China cannot compete effectively with the United States on innovation that builds directly on breakthroughs in the basic sciences, unless these countries dramatically change their basic science infrastructure. To be fair, China is attempting this, but India is not. Still, even China is years, if not decades, behind in its innovation-supporting infrastructure.

Nor can these countries yet compete directly on high-value-added innovations introduced by companies to generate a profit; these innovations require a deep understanding of developed markets populated by rich customers. When Apple's iPad appeared in 2010, the consumer frenzy led to the purchase of about one million iPads within twenty-eight days of its launch in the U.S. market.[4] The iPad was not a new product developed from careful market research, but instead was invented to satisfy unarticulated consumer needs. Buyers in the United States thus paid $499 for a basic version, even though most of them already owned a $1,000-plus laptop computer and a $100-plus mobile smart phone, for which they might pay $100 or more per month to ensure a constant Internet connection. Here again, the West and companies from the developed markets enjoy an advantage over other companies in terms of igniting consumers' desires for innovative products, regardless of cost. Indian and Chinese companies must struggle constantly to devise products that might appeal to these consumers who are so far removed from the physical, economic, emotional, and experiential realities of their own domestic markets.

In contrast with iPad's universe of affluent consumers, consider the larger world of budget-constrained consumers in India, for whom the mobile phone is the technology device of choice and necessity. The enormity of five billion mobile phone subscriptions worldwide suggests that more people have access to cell phones than to clean toilets in countries like India. In India, telecommunication companies such as Bharti Airtel and Reliance Communications routinely sell handsets that cost less than $20 and connect to the network with no monthly charges. One-cent-per-minute phone calls, one-cent text messages, and cheap access to the Web provide tickets to a world full of possibilities.

The differences between the expensive iPad and cheap mobile phone services illuminate the different trajectories of developed and emerging markets. The developed world's consumer technology innovations are built for an ever-expanding bandwidth network and move toward fancier, costlier, and more network-hungry and status-conferring devices. In emerging markets, firms constantly seek new uses for cheap, basic innovations, such as those that allow people to use their mobile phones for banking, weather forecasts, market reports, and employment prospects.

Global leadership in an industry often results from the presence of demanding domestic consumers. Japanese consumers are extremely demanding when it comes to electronics, German consumers when it comes to automobiles, Americans when it comes to fast-food products, and French and Italian consumers when it comes to fashion. It is not a coincidence that leading domestic companies exist in these industries. A similar dynamic is alive and well in India, where innovation is a direct response to the needs of the Indian marketplace, in which consumers are both demanding and budget con-strained. Anandh Balasundaram, the managing director at AstraZeneca India, described the difference between Western and Indian consumers:

> Indian consumers are a lot more value conscious than anywhere I've seen. I think we always viewed it as being cost conscious, but I see it as value. They really dig into the details of what value is by asking, 'How is this prod-uct going to change my life?' Consumers in the U.S., for example, will spend ten dollars to try something out. But Indian consumers, they'll ask hundreds of questions—will it do this? will it handle that?—and they ask, 'Do I really need it?' before they spend even a small amount. So as a marketer to the Indian consumer, this constant value con-sciousness requires us to think hard in terms of what is the value added, as well as the differentiation you are bringing to the marketplace.

According to Guillermo Wille, managing director at General Electric in India, "the beauty of the Indian market is that it pushes you in a corner . . . it demands everything in the world, but cheaper and smaller." In other words, India's budget-constrained customers have allowed the emergence of capa-bilities for a certain kind of innovation in India. Tata Motor's launch of the Nano, the cheapest car in the world to make, is a prime example.

The Nano Effect

With a vision to mass manufacture "the people's car," Tata Motors set out to design the least expensive production car in the world for less than 100,000 rupees (about US$2,500).[5] When the Nano launched in late 2009, it made headlines around the globe and was heralded as a new breed of transportation. Think of it: an Indian company was at the forefront of a sea change in one of the largest industries in the world and was leading the market for smaller, lighter, cheaper cars.

Tata Motors initially developed the Nano to meet a real domestic need. Two-wheelers—with the father driving, an older child standing in front, and the wife sitting in the back holding a baby—were the norm, but also a relatively unsafe mode of transportation. Ratan Tata, the chairman of Tata Group, wanted safer but still affordable forms of transportation. Although it began with the idea of rebuilding cars around the scooter, the company's thinking evolved and gravitated toward something more carlike but revolutionary.

The price point was not the initial focus. The notion that it could be a 100,000-rupee car emerged when, in an interview at the Geneva Car Show, Ratan Tata tossed out this off-the-cuff response. Tata then took this number back to India and presented it to his team as a target price. The developers, understandably, were aghast. But they also did their best to deliver. Their first challenge was to reduce production costs by radically decreasing the car's performance but still meeting the needs of Indian drivers. Every element of the car was questioned, from door handles to engine placement to the location of the instrument cluster. The result of this exercise?

A rear-mounted pressure-die-cast engine, wheels that sit at the extremities, and a single windshield wiper (among other things). Finally, Tata came up with an innovative distribution model that would lower costs because it sold the automobile in kits to dealer-entrepreneurs who assembled them for buyers.

As a potential model, Tata referred to the Swiss Swatch, a product introduced with a disruptively low price that dominated its niche but did not undermine the overall watch market. Tata aimed to cannibalize some of the lower-end car market and some of the higher-end motorcycle and scooter market, as well as create a market of its own. In India, the Nano offers a high level of quality to millions who thought safe transportation was beyond their reach. In countries more developed, the Nano could appeal to consumers' expanding appetite for small cars.

Beyond innovating a new product and a new sales method, Tata proved unequivocally with its Nano that there was tremendous opportunity in designing a product for the low-income market. The actual technology and the materials used in its construction had been available for years, but it took an Indian company that focused on the demands of its domestic market to produce such an innovation. Although perhaps the best known of these innovations outside India, the Nano is not the only example of this type of globally visible innovation to emerge from India.

The Council of Scientific and Industrial Research's Soleckshaw is a state-of-the-art, solar-powered version of the humble cycle rickshaw. With its top speed of fifteen kilometers per hour (just under ten miles per hour), the Soleckshaw also boasts a sturdier frame than most rickshaws on India's roads and spring-loaded foam seats that can hold up to three people. A fully charged solar battery gives it power for up to seventy kilometers (just over forty miles), and its structure was developed specifically for India's urban streets, with their tight mazes of narrow alleys and winding streets, choked with buses, cars, scooters, and cyclists, as well as bustling pedestrians. The Soleckshaw offers an effective solution to traffic woes, chronic pollution, and fossil-fuel dependence (not to mention relief from back-breaking work for the rickshaw driver). This innovation appears to be just the beginning; an advanced version with a carlike body may offer a viable alternative to small cars. And why not? The conveyance might have been built with urban India in mind, but a company that provides viable green transportation stands to gain tremendous rewards from eco-conscious consumers in any setting.

First-World Technology at Third-World Prices

Leading MNCs, including GE, Intel, Microsoft, Philips, Siemens, and Xerox, all recognize India's unique innovation capabilities for income-constrained consumers. Indian consumers want first-world technology at third-world prices, so products developed for India probably can find markets in other emerging countries in Asia, Africa, and Latin America, where consumers have similar needs. Budget-constrained segments in developed markets also find such products appealing. Pioneering MNCs, therefore, installed resources in India to develop products for the domestic Indian market and married them with global processes to transfer the newly developed products to the rest of the world. As Vijay Govindarajan at Dartmouth has documented, this process actually reverses MNCs' traditional logic, in which they developed products to meet the requirements of consumers in the developed world and then localized them for emerging markets.[6]

GE's Portable Electrocardiograph

The reversal is evident in GE's success with portable electrocardiograph (ECG) machines.[7] Traditional ECG units that GE and its competitors imported into India were large and expensive, so only leading Indian urban hospitals could afford them— even though the vast majority of India's population lives in rural areas and could not travel easily to urban diagnostic centers. For its MAC 400 and 400i models of the ECG, GE instead developed designs in its Bengaluru-based R&D facility and then manufactured the frugally designed portable devices in India using local components. Although the primary target market was impoverished rural Indian patients, with minimal access to electricity and poor transportation links, the models have now moved into developed markets.

The handheld MAC 400i is about the size of a credit card reader and weighs less than a kilogram. It runs on a small laptop with batteries but can record one hundred ECGs on a single charge. At launch, it cost $500, compared with $1,000 for its predecessor (MAC 400) and $3,000 for an imported machine. It also reduced the cost of a test to $0.20—from $50! Such an offering is especially appealing in a country where the majority of the patients are not only poor but also constrained by a pay-as-you-go health-care model.

An adapted MAC 400 appeared in the United States in 2009; the introduction of the adapted machine represented another innovation for GE. In the United States, developing an ECG machine from scratch could take GE Healthcare five years and cost as much as $2 million. Although GE Healthcare dominated the U.S. market with its big-ticket diagnostic machines and sold 34 percent of the ECG machines used in hospitals and clinics, the company also recognized a market for smaller machines. Focus groups across the United States led to the relatively quick and inexpensive development of the MAC 800, which is basically the same model with a few new features, such as a USB drive, Ethernet, and telephone ports to upload patient data. Thus, the company slashed its U.S. development costs to $225,000 and decreased the time to market to a few months, but still offered the latest technology in a unit that weighed just six pounds, half as much as the smallest ECG machine available for sale at the time. The machine itself cost $2,500, an 80 percent markdown from products with similar capabilities. The smaller, cheaper machine was pitched mainly to a new medical market, such as primary-care doctors, rural clinics, and visiting nurses who needed a device they could easily tote (and afford).

Philips's SMILE Initiative

The GE success story may make it seem simple. But MNCs continue to struggle to develop innovations for low-income customers in India and transfer them to other markets, because the very process challenges global companies' established practices. For example, the SMILE (Sustainable Model in Lighting Everywhere) initiative by Philips, to create sustainable off-grid lighting solutions for people without access to electricity, demonstrates the dilemmas companies face.[8]

At the end of 2004, as part of a corporate push to develop products for impoverished markets, the Dutch electronics company Philips formed an Indo-Dutch team to understand Indian consumers' lighting needs. The team soon discovered limited markets for existing Philips products: few Indian consumers in rural areas had access to electricity, and those in urban areas faced frequent power outages. Kerosene lanterns provided a popular (if imperfect and dangerous) substitute. So Philips developed several product concepts for testing with Indian consumers; two made it to the market in 2006. Kiran, a hand-cranked flashlight, used long-lasting light-emitting diodes (LEDs) and targeted users with no access to electricity. Uday, a rechargeable, portable lantern that Philips later modified to use solar power, targeted middle-class users with erratic access to the power supply. Solar lighting, especially compared with kerosene, offered cost savings, reduced risk of fire, smaller carbon footprints, and the use of a sustainable, natural commodity (i.e., sunlight) to generate electricity.

Despite all this promise, Philips still struggled to turn its innovations into sustainable businesses. The Uday lamp started out at a cost of $37, which Philips believed was appropriate because Indian consumers typically spent between $35 and $42 per year on lighting from kerosene lanterns and candles. But the real problem was accessibility; to get the product in the hands of rural consumers, Philips developed new distribution channels, including the use of women's self-help groups and local nongovernmental organizations.

Then, market tests showed Philips that few rural consumers needed as much light as the two products provided. So next it developed less expensive, affordable products with less light intensity. As Unmesh Kulkarni, senior design manager for the Pune-based Philips division, observed, "Designing for simple solutions at the lowest possible cost is in many ways more challenging than designing a very advanced, high-tech solution."[9] One may add that it is even easier when the customers don't face harsh budget constraints. Simona Rocchi, director of sustainable design at Philips Design in the Netherlands, concurred: "It's not about taking older, cheaper products and technology to emerging markets, . . . it's about taking a new technology and adapting it in smart ways to allow people . . . to leapfrog into the latest in lighting—LED."[10] Six years after the Philips mandate went out, the two products have yet to become major sellers, even as Philips continues to hope for their success.

In 2008, Philips moved the SMILE project to Ghana, in collaboration with the Dutch government, the international development organization World Vision, and local Ghanaian nongovernmental organizations. The goal in this case was to ensure that ten million people in sub-Saharan African countries would have access to renewable energy lighting solutions by 2015. Adaptations of Uday for Africa included testing to determine whether people preferred a central solar panel as a charging station rather than a small, attached solar panel. In this case, the MNC is combining traditional with new innovation paths: Philips is innovating in a developing market, but is still adjusting the innovation to meet the needs of different consumers in other developing markets.

Philips also hopes to market the low-cost, solar-powered, Indian-innovated lighting system to the West. Selling emerging-market hand-me-ups in developed markets carries risks, though. The less expensive products may cannibalize sales of higher-priced goods with better margins. Thus, Gerard J. Kleisterlee, CEO of Philips, refrained from introducing the less expensive products into developed markets, to protect the company's existing product line and out of concern of "hurting margins if you go too far down."[11]

Frugal Engineering: India's Engine for Visible Innovation

The invisible innovations discussed in chapters 2 through 5 were all triggered by the availability of highly skilled employees at low prices in India (budget-conserving talent). In contrast, visible innovations from India like Nano or GE's new ECG machine are catalyzed by the need to serve markets with low purchasing power (budget-constrained customers, though undoubtedly, the budget-conserving talent helps to make these innovations possible). However, there is more to this approach than just making things cheaper. Carlos Ghoshn, who heads Renault-Nissan, is credited with coining the term *frugal engineering* to signify achieving more with fewer resources.[12] Frugal engineering is not mere *jugaad*, that is, making fixes and finding work-arounds. Whereas *jugaads*—while undoubtedly creative and inventive—essentially signal resignation to current constraints, frugal engineering can be a systematic approach to making those constraints irrelevant, or at least less important. As many are beginning to recognize, excessive dependence on the *jugaad* mind-set may in fact impede the ability to fundamentally transform a situation through disciplined engineering, frugal or otherwise.[13]

Frugal engineering is very much a child of its context. Its development has been intimately tied to the brute fact of low purchasing power among the vast majority of Indian consumers. At the same time, the fruits of frugal engineering could well be valued outside India and, in our view, may be the basis on which Indian innovation gains global visibility.

For instance, when Armin Bruck, managing director of Siemens in India, set out to convince the German engineering company's board of the potential for Indian innovation, he gave the board members the keys to a Tata Nano.[14] He wanted to convey the smell and feel of a revolutionary mass-market product and persuade them to improve the pipeline of local inventions aimed at Indian consumers. Peter Löscher, the company's chief executive, and his colleagues Heinrich Heisinger and Joe Kaeser piled into the world's cheapest car and drove around New Delhi. The test drive fortified the company's effort to reconfigure its strategy to develop high-quality engineering technology for low-cost emerging markets.

Another MNC has employed frugal engineering in a much more modest product. For many years, Nestlé sold its Maggi brand dried noodles only to rural Pakistan and India, for about twenty cents per serving.[15] In 2008, the company began promoting Maggi in Australia and New Zealand as a budget-friendly health food with no oil, less salt, and no monosodium glutamate.

Siemens, the German engineering giant, discovered that developing a low-cost X-ray machine for India helped improve its models sold in Europe and the United States. While trying to frugally engineer an X-ray machine for operating theaters in its Indian R&D center, the company found that the camera at the core of the machine could be produced for about $500, as opposed to $2,000 in the Western models. "The new camera is not a cheap copy of a Western model," said Vishnu

The Pillars of Frugal Engineering

The instances of frugal engineering we analyzed during our research suggest that this type of innovation can be a distinctive paradigm for new product development, with a distinctive set of dimensions on which success is measured, and a related set of underlying capabilities. We outline these briefly in the following paragraphs.

Robustness

Robustness in product design refers to stability in the face of variations in the operating environment. India is a harsh environment in terms of the huge variances that occur in operating conditions, and that setting affects the priorities that drive product development and innovation. As Wille of GE explained, "We design products that are robust to the Indian environment." This means not just extremes of temperature, but erratic electricity supplies and peak-load ratios unheard-of in the West. For example, when designing its milk- or juice-packaging machines for India and other emerging markets, Tetra Pak has to recognize that the necessary inputs of compressed air, electricity, and chilled water as well as the operator skills will be a challenge in terms of quality and consistency, yet the packaging solution must work.

To take another instance, Nokia has gained a dominant share of the Indian market and has hired more people in India than in any other country except for its home base of Finland. Each of Nokia's three Indian R&D centers is an integral part of the firm's global R&D infrastructure. Product features developed for the Indian market include a dust-proof keypad and face, a torch light, and nonslip sides for better grip during humidity—the bane of the monsoon season—all features that a Finnish inventor in stable, cool Nordic conditions might never imagine.

Think of the Nano's ability to navigate Indian roads, or the MAC 400i's capacity to function in a dusty dot in the hinterland, and you get the sense of how robust these designs have had to be.

Portability

Rather than expecting the rural population to travel to urban centers, many innovators believe that services must be taken to the people. Space constraints and the need to transport products to rural areas over poor transportation links highlight the importance of portability in India. Small and lightweight become highly desirable product attributes. Think again of the MAC 400i ECG, and consider the miniaturization efforts that are necessary to achieve this kind of portability in a product class that typically sets no value on portability at all.

Defeaturing

Defeaturing consists of feature rationalization, or "ditching the junk DNA" that tends to accumulate in products over time. With Indian consumers, firms can avoid implementing features that do little to enhance the actual product. As V. Raja, chief executive of GE Healthcare for South Asia observed, "For something to work in India, you don't need all the bells and whistles."[16] Wille of GE agreed: "In addition to

(continued)

The Pillars of Frugal Engineering (continued)

portability and robustness, it's necessary to refocus features. Say a standard version at use in other parts of the world has ten features, but the Indian consumers and clients ask, 'Do we really need all ten, or can they be reduced to the two or three that are truly essential?'"

Siemens supports its innovation efforts in India with a billion-euro investment devoted entirely to developing and adapting products for the local market. Currently, Siemens employs seventeen thousand people who work on forty-two products that eventually will be sold in India and exported to other markets. Most of the prototypes are held in strict secrecy, but leaks hint at the possibility of solar-powered X-ray machines, fetal heart monitors, steam turbines, and road traffic management systems. The CEO of Siemens, Peter Löscher, alluded to the change in mind-set: "These products require a different kind of innovation. What counts here is simplicity, not sophistication."[17]

Leapfrog Technology

It may seem contradictory, but some infrastructure gaps in India have positively affected Indian innovation: they have forced entrepreneurs and companies to adopt technologies that make reliance on existing infrastructure (creaking and unreliable as it is in many ways) simply irrelevant. Praveen Vishakantaiah, president of Intel India, called India "a fantastic place where, when it comes to product innovation, you can actually jump over what's out there." Indian engineers have invented a battery-powered, ultra-low-cost refrigerator resistant to power cuts; an automatic teller machine for rural areas; and even a flour mill powered by a scooter. People in the West, with its constant access to electricity, have little motivation to pursue such innovations. But once these innovations are developed, consider the possible applications to disaster relief, low-population-density areas, or outdoor leisure activities in Western markets.

The Indian mobile phone industry is the poster child for leapfrogging over infrastructural constraints. A limited fixed-line infrastructure created an opportunity for mobile phones to reach many more people. Mobile telephony is also relatively cheap, sharable, and easily repaired. And thus, a new frontier of global innovation opened in India. Mobile phones are used for everything. Need a job? Use your phone to look for one. Wondering about the background of that politician? Get text messages with detailed information about him or her. Xerox has hired innovation managers to search for inventions and products emerging from Indian mobile telephony related start-ups that Xerox could adapt, and Hewlett-Packard is using its Indian research lab to test whether it can use Web-interface applications for mobile phones in developed markets.

Megascale Production

With its massive population, India has market segments that if captured, can help firms drive costs down through production at massive scale—megaproduction. For example, the 1996 development of antiretroviral drugs in the West helped reduce the death rates of HIV/AIDS patients by 84 percent

(continued)

The Pillars of Frugal Engineering (continued)

within four years. But the annual cost of $10,000 to $15,000 for this medication made this treatment far too expensive for India and other emerging markets. Then Cipla introduced its generic version of the treatment in 2001 for $350 per year, and Ranbaxy followed shortly thereafter with a version for $295 per year. The treatments' low prices depended partly on their large-scale production in India (but also, admittedly, on the companies' ability to circumvent years of R&D)—a tactic particularly prominent in India's extensive exporting of generic drugs to low- and middle-income countries. The costs of component manufacturing for the Nano, for alternative energy products, or for mobile handsets in India similarly reflect the scale at which these products can be produced.

Service Ecosystems

The conventional wisdom in marketing is that reaching demanding cost targets requires low variability, or a one-size-fits-all mentality. Selling large volumes requires that a product appeal to multiple segments, each with slightly different needs. An irreconcilable dilemma? In fact it is another route for innovation by Indian firms, which resolve the dilemma by using efficient service ecosystems. These ecosystems achieve low

---

Swaminathan, head of the embedded hardware system program at Siemens Corporate Technology India. "We redesigned everything from scratch with a view to cutting costs while meeting the specific needs of local doctors." Since the new camera is much cheaper but comparable to the original ver-

costs, but also highlight product features and thus broaden the product's appeal. For example, Cummins Engine Company of India developed a modular, low-horsepower diesel engine that could be combined with distributors' accessories.[18] The version designed for hospitals thus incorporated a noise-abatement hood, while the one directed toward farmers could feature dust guard and dirt guard add-ons.

Today, it is easy to see a plethora of small repair shops and other businesses that have mushroomed around population centers in India. The use of these service ecosystems—which comprise not just parts and repair but financing as well—can help firms enlarge their product markets. For example, Selco, which designs simple, low-cost systems that combine solar panels and storage batteries, has installed solar lighting systems in a hundred thousand homes in rural southern India.[19] A two-light home system can cost around $200, or 10,000 rupees—expensive, considering that the company's customers earn less than half that in a month. So Selco assembled an aggressive financing package with various local rural banks that provide financing to 85 percent of Selco customers; the repayment rate for solar loans is about 90 percent. In addition, service support personnel visit customers once every three months during the first year to ensure that the system is working properly and to collect batteries for recycling.

sion in quality, it makes sense to install it in the models aimed at developed markets.[20]

The general principle is simple—the fundamental rethink of a product that accompanies frugal engineering efforts in an emerging market may throw up solutions that are also valuable in developed markets. It should not be surprising that cutting-edge innovation in mobile phone services, alternate energy generation, and cheap mass transport may come from countries like India and China.

Reva Electric Car Company in Bengaluru suggests this type of global potential. Its agile two-seater, called the REVAi, has been well received outside its home market. For example, in London (where the car sells as G-Wiz), a standard model costs around £10,000. Because it is an electrically propelled vehicle, G-Wiz is exempt from the London congestion charge, which prohibits most drivers from keeping a car, and parking it is free. Drivers in other European countries have found ways to buy the REVAi; new markets have sprung up in Spain and Norway, as well as on other continents, such as in Costa Rica and Brazil. General Motors agreed to license technology from Reva for its Spark car, which it planned to launch in Indian and U.S. markets. However, Reva was acquired by Mahindra & Mahindra in 2010, and GM ended its relationship with Reva soon after—which may tell us something about the seriousness with which GM views Mahindra & Mahindra as a competitor.

Recommendations

Innovation in India may not be powered by breakthroughs in basic science or conducted for consumers with big wallets and a taste for novelty, until India's science infrastructure and the purchasing power of Indian consumers improves dramatically. However, the innovation that does occur in India is conducted in a context that makes frugal product development practices as natural as breathing—and it is conducted for a group of consumers who are in the fastest-growing segments in the world. Thus, success in Indian visible innovation may come largely from frugal engineering for budget-constrained consumers, just as much of Indian invisible innovation may come from budget-conserving talent available at a scale un-heard-of in most other parts of the world. So what does this mean for managers and policy makers?

- MNCs stand to benefit by tapping into Indian frugal engineering:

  - The resulting innovations can be offered in India as a complete product line to meet the needs of different segments of consumers.

  - The innovations can be offered in other budget-constrained, emerging markets.

  - The MNCs gain unique offerings for budget-constrained niche segments in developed markets.

  - The innovations can be used to help improve and simplify products that are currently offered to high-end consumers of the developed markets (but see the next point as well).

- Western policy makers should consider how frugal engineering practices may help to provide cost efficient public services—in health care, for instance.

- Best practices in frugal engineering are unlikely to come from a textbook. It is up to sophisticated Indian engineers and managers in companies to create a set of standards, a body of knowledge, and a community of practitioners around the concept, much as it has been created for quality management or the Toyota production system. Policy makers in India can help encourage research and training in codified frugal-engineering practices, once these have developed sufficiently. Indian companies and MNCs operating in India need to leverage the capability that the country is developing for frugal engineering. These capabilities enable product development with the following features:

- Develop product robustness to harsh and varying operating conditions.

- Work on portability to move solutions to people in remote and poorly connected areas.

- Defeature products to reduce junk DNA of products and to begin design afresh.

- Leapfrog technology to make existing infrastructural constraints irrelevant.

- Use megascale production to drive down costs.

- Develop service ecosystems to help economically customize products and related services.

7 India's Innovation Challenge
Overcoming Institutional Constraints

I N MANY WAYS, India has begun to evolve from a leader in the services outsourcing sector to an innovation destination. Yet, it would be foolhardy to minimize the considerable challenges that still confront the country on its journey to becoming a global innovation hub.

To be clear, we are not speaking here of the problems of basic infrastructure: sanitation, health, and poverty—enormously important as they are. We are not even speaking about the general business climate—which remains dismal with India ranked 134th out of 183 countries in The World Bank's 2011 ease of "Doing Business" report.[1] The cost and complexity of dispute settlement and contract enforcement is especially poor as on the enforcing contracts dimension, India ranked 182 out of 183 countries! The presence of these general infrastructure limitations noted above has not prevented undisputed global leaders in the software development and back-office services from emerging in India. The generally poor state of Indian infrastructure has ultimately had little to do with the world-class facilities that an Infosys and a TCS, or the Indian School of Business, have been able to assemble, albeit within a cocoon. Undoubtedly, building and sustaining such facilities without the aid of good infrastructure imposes higher operating costs than would be the case if the public infrastructure were robust. However, to the extent that India's compensating advantages such as lower labor costs and larger labor pools have remained, the overall effects on business strategy have been insignificant. The implication for public policy—in particular, for equitable growth and political stability—is another, quite troubling issue altogether.[2]

Rather, our specific focus here is on the considerable challenges facing some of the key institutional pillars of innovation. The concept of National Systems of Innovation helps explain the institutional enablers and impediments to innovativeness in a country.[3] In essence, the idea is that the capacity for innovation in any economy depends on multiple factors and interactions between multiple players, some of which could be shaped actively by direct or indirect government intervention. Accordingly, we have selected aspects of the institutional environment that we believe are critical to developing both visible and invisible innovation in India, and the weaknesses therein. While we point out important corrective action that the private sector has already begun taking in some of these areas, we also highlight the critical role for public policy.

In particular, we focus on the talent pipeline, the intellectual property (IP) regime, and the venture capital sector within the innovation system of India. Although other elements are also important, these three are critical and are under the most pressure. If these pillars of innovation can be strengthened, India's trajectory toward becoming a globally important source of innovation is secure. Instead, if they crumble, the trajectory will remain an unfulfilled promise.

The Mirage of Mighty Labor Pools

The heart of India's innovation potential beats because of constant infusions of talent. India and China are neck and neck in the race to be the world's most populous nation; it seems likely that by 2050, India will take the lead.[4] For now, India constitutes one-third of the world's low-cost labor supply. In addition, more than half the population—in excess of 500 million people—are under the age of twenty-five years, and in the next five years (2011–2015), Indians will come to account for nearly one-quarter of the increase in people of working age on the planet.

And yet, India's seemingly vast ocean of human resources represents barely a ripple in the pool of skilled talent necessary for innovation. Estimates place the Indian R&D talent pool at between 100,000 and 300,000 people, compared with, for example, 925,000 in China, 477,000 in Russia, and 150,000 in Korea.[5] In terms of the level of education needed at the front lines of innovation, India produced about 6,600 science and technology (S&T) PhDs in 2007, compared with 8,000 in China and 12,000 in the United States in 2003.[6] India's share of the world's technical talent pool is thus significant but not dominant.

Only about 10 percent of the college-aged population (aged eighteen to twenty-four) attends college in India, compared with 20 percent in China and 60 percent in the United States. Even the flagship institutions in India's educational firmament—the Indian Institutes of Technology (IITs) and Indian Institutes of Management—are notoriously understaffed and operate as much as one-third below their sanctioned faculty strength.[7] These indicators forewarn a dangerous shortage of skilled talent in the next generation; the shortage already manifests itself in the sharp annual compensation increases and employee turnover rates in India. Simply put, increases in India's skilled workforce are inadequate to support India's growth.

To illustrate this crisis, consider two specific sectors. For semiconductors, Rahul Bedi from Intel India estimates that about fifteen or sixteen PhDs (of interest to Intel) come out of the country in one year; the country itself produces less than a thousand engineering PhDs.[8] For pharmaceutical R&D, the near future will be marked by significant talent shortfalls in the needed numbers of biologists, medicinal chemists, and clinical investigators.[9] Tanjore Balganesh, head of the Indian R&D lab of AstraZeneca, emphasized the shortage of medicinal chemistry skills:

During a brainstorming session, there might be a room full of seventy-five people, all contributing, but there's not a single chemist. We are trying to do drug discovery without a chemist! Biologists think they can make a drug on their own, but the reality is, a biologist cannot; it's the chemists who make a drug, and in India, there just aren't that many medicinal chemists. Why not? Here is what I think is the root cause: medicinal chemistry is biology, mathematics, and chemistry put together. Yet the educational system [in India] is such that by the ninth standard, most students have to make a hard and irreversible choice between mathematics and biology.

In a country the size of India, it is difficult to imagine that the total output of PhDs across a number of scientific fields is about the same as the number emerging from a single good S&T university in the United States! The Indian university system is not only failing to train, but also, at a more fundamental level, failing to create new knowledge and innovation. As described in chapter 2, one of us conducted a study with Suma Athreye of Brunel University to examine all patents granted by the U.S. Patent and Trademark Office between 1976 and 2006, in which at least one of the patent authors had an Indian or Chinese address.[10] Indian universities are practically invisible in this patenting data. We found that noncorporate patenting in the USPTO from India is dominated by the Council for Scientific and Industrial Research (CSIR), a network of thirty-seven government-funded research institutes whose mandate (as implied in the name) is industrial innovation, rather than training or basic research. However, in many fields, particularly those related to chemistry, basic research is represented, if at all, primarily by CSIR rather than the universities. In contrast, Chinese universities had a healthy though small patenting presence across a range of sectors.

Research Productivity in India:
The Case of Management Knowledge

We took a close look at India in a field of academic research that we know something about: management research. In 1961, the Indian government set up Indian Institutes of Management (IIMs) at Ahmedabad and Kolkata. In 1973, another IIM was added in Bengaluru. Given that essentially, the three IIMs along with a few lesser-ranked private institutions dominated the Indian business school landscape until the 1980s, the competition to obtain admission into the IIMs was intense. This selection effect of choosing a few hundred students from hundreds of thousands of applicants ensured that the graduating class was exceptional, quite independent of any "processing" effect during the program. Not surprisingly, the IIMs have become very famous for their alumni. Observing the success of the IIMs and the huge demand for MBA degrees, private entrepreneurs have stepped in, especially in the past two decades, to set up business schools. Wikipedia now claims that there are twenty-five hundred business schools in India, and we see more are emerging every week.

Yet, while Indian business schools may be teaching exceptionally motivated students, we see little evidence that faculty are creating innovative ideas through research. To assess the state of management research in India, we examined data on authorship of research by India-based authors for the period 1990 to 2009. We chose the list of forty journals that the *Financial Times* used for ranking research at business schools around the world in its MBA rankings (www.ft.com). Using the ISI Web of Science database for this period, we tracked down all journal articles that listed at least one author with an affiliation to an Indian institution. We then computed the Indian "author count" for each article. For instance, for an article with three authors, one of whom was based in India, we counted the author appearance as one. If all three authors were based in India, the score would have been three.

Over these two decades, the total number of Indian author counts was 132 (108 unique articles, or about five articles per year for the entire country). This is not an impressive number by the standards even of a single leading global business school. For example, schools such as Hong Kong University of Science and Technology (about 100-plus faculty members) currently produce more than thirty articles annually, while a larger business school like Wharton (200-plus faculty) produces about twice as many articles. However, there are some interesting and encouraging signs.

First, in the 1990s, the most productive Indian institutions for business research were not business schools but instead the Indian Statistical Institutes in Kolkata and New Delhi. However, in the 2000 decade, the business schools had clearly taken the lead, with Indian School of Business (ISB) at Hyderabad and the IIMs at Bengaluru and Kolkata doing well.

Second, amazingly, a new school—ISB—has managed to wrest a leadership position in research, despite having published its first article in our sample in 2003! In our view, the aspiration to build a world-class research culture, and

(continued)

Research Productivity in India:
The Case of Management Knowledge (continued)

substantial investments in infrastructure and faculty salaries at the ISB, has created this intellectual advantage. Nevertheless, IIMs Bengaluru and Kolkata have also done well so far, despite the absence of such advantages. Perhaps there are multiple models to improve research productivity in Indian universities—and not all of them may be equally expensive.

Recent data suggests that if anything, the Chinese university system has gone from strength to strength, and the country now produces research articles in international journals at a volume second only to the United States (which China is expected to overtake soon).[11] Research productivity in India has also improved but remains patchy—with pockets of excellence within some of the IITs, the Indian Institute of Science, and some of the CSIR network of laboratories, but with the university system largely not participating.

The quantity shortfall is not the only concern; a lack of *quality* in India's talent pool has also proved problematic. We spoke with many R&D managers of MNC subsidiaries who confessed that only a small proportion of the people who graduated in their disciplines were actually employable. At the university undergraduate level, the global consulting firm McKinsey & Company estimates this small proportion to be below 30 percent.[12] Graduates' inability to perform on the job was no less striking at higher levels of education. NASSCOM, an organization that represents the Indian software industry, estimates that upward of 50 percent of S&T graduates in India cannot function effectively in software-oriented jobs. These estimates are based on varied notions, though, because standards are uneven across the board. The top seven Indian IITs, established in the 1940s by Prime Minister Jawaharlal Nehru to educate engineers for public works projects, unquestionably deserve their global reputation but produce only eight thousand graduates in India each year.[13]

The dearth of PhDs has created a severe upstream constraint as well: faculty who can teach the next generation of S&T graduates. A 2007 World Bank report estimates that 20–30 percent of lecturer and professor positions in Indian universities and institutes are vacant.[14] Retaining high-quality S&T graduates in academia is difficult, because industry offers nearly irresistible lures, including much higher salaries and the prestige of working for some of the world's best corporate labs—in India.

Historically, large numbers of graduates from the best institutes left India annually, taking their foundational knowledge with them. Many remain abroad today, not only to take advantage of the opportunities for promising careers in leading-edge MNCs but also to make more money than they possibly could in India. Contributing to this problem is a lack of public spending on higher education back home, a responsibility of India's central and state governments. Compared with higher education spending in the United States (2.6 percent), Japan (3.4 percent), and China (1.3 percent), India spends just 0.6 percent of its gross domestic product on education. In addition, strict government oversight means that universities lack the fiscal, managerial, or curriculum autonomy needed to excel.

There are some promising signs of change. In late 2009, for example, India's central government allowed the CSIR's Advanced Institute of Science and Technology to become an autonomous university. The step allows the institute to develop courses explicitly designed to prepare graduates for the real world; according to Samir Brahmachari, the director general of CSIR, it will offer undergraduate and postgraduate courses in fields such as abrasion engineering and fabrionics, courses "that have never been offered in India before." Brahmachari continued: "Five hundred faculty will be drawn from the best of Indian industry, and another five hundred will represent the top Indian S&T professors." Recent legislation is also making it easier for foreign universities to set up campuses in India. Interestingly, Indian institutes are, for the first time, also actively seeking to hire foreign nationals, including professors of Indian origin, to teach in India.

But perhaps the most interesting initiatives are emerging from the private sector, in which several players effectively "backward-integrate" themselves into the production of their own talent. Almost every large Indian IT player, from Infosys to Tata Consultancy Services to Wipro, is enthusiastically collaborating with universities to supply course materials and trained lecturers who teach about the topics most relevant to their business, whether that material pertains to chip design or radio-frequency identification. These companies also have robust in-house training for their new hires. For example, the Wipro Academy of Software Excellence runs its own four-year (part-time) graduate master's program in software engineering, and Infosys has a world-class campus in Mysore to train forty thousand new recruits annually.

According to Praveen Vishakantaiah, who leads Intel's R&D operations in India, the company's management recognized early that "we have to help solve the problem. We've got to expand the base which you can hire from . . . and that's a multiyear program." He went on to explain how Intel planned to enlarge the pool of skilled talent for its specific research agenda in India:

First, we identified a few areas where we believe there is a lack of skilled talent; we identified the B-tech or M-tech [business technology or management technology] curriculum as typically out of sync with the reality of the Indian environment. So what we did is that we worked closely with universities. We have created an alliance with IIT Kanpur as a think tank for developing courses on multicore processors, for example. Because what we realized is that while [we], AMD, and the whole gang [are] coming out with multicore processors, PhD graduates have no clue; . . . they have no clue how to develop on it. So if the next generation of innovators can't use it, what's the point of making this, right? So we asked how to design a curriculum that exposes students to concepts such as this. Last term we had about two-hundred-plus colleges across the country which were looking into and adopting this curriculum.

How could Intel manage to organize and roll out such a huge project—not to mention pay for it? Intel's Rahul Bedi explained: "Obviously, we can't go train everybody, so we'll adopt a 'train-the-trainer approach' with master faculty trainers, on a cascading delivery system. A tier-one college will train its tier-two brother . . . and so on." Intel quickly discovered that working with state-run universities was a deep challenge, so to overcome tight controls on its curriculum, Intel often starts with electives. Bedi described the process: "What happens is that many universities have their own board of school studies, which meets every few years. If any particular elective course becomes popular with the students, that's when the faculty can go to the board and potentially say, 'Guys, students love it, let's formalize this in the curriculum.' So that's how it percolates; it takes a while."

Following another path, AstraZeneca made a major grant to IIT Chennai to develop a Department of Medicinal Chemistry. According to Anandh Balasundaram, who leads AstraZeneca's Indian operations, the firm hopes "that within five years, we will start to see more talent emerge." The company has also launched courses on process chemistry at Bangalore University, assigning the company's scientists to serve as visiting faculty. The AstraZeneca Research Foundation India also regularly organizes seminars, symposia, and workshops on cutting-edge biomedical and pharmaceutical science subjects to support both education and technological innovation in these areas.

The beneficiaries of this backward integration by corporations into talent production are not just the IITs. India also has about two thousand state-run vocational training centers, known as Industrial Training Institutes. The curricula in these institutes are archaic, and less than half the students actually find jobs on graduation. However, many corporates such as Mafatlal Denim, Hero Honda, Tata Motors, and Ispat Steel have begun to "adopt" individual institutes to try to make them more relevant to modern industry.[15]

Beyond training new talent, many companies also hunt actively for repats (returning global Indians), a step that would enable these companies to tap into a huge talent pool of skilled Indians working abroad. Guillermo Wille, head of the

John F. Welch Technology Centre, said that GE India "goes to look for" Indians abroad. He noted that GE India went to "practically all the big technical universities in the world" to persuade the best Indian scientists to return. His explanation of how he accomplished it is instructive: "Basically, every member of my staff is responsible for fostering a relationship with several universities abroad. And so, whenever we go, to the UK or to Europe or to America or Australia, we visit those universities, and we talk to the Indian population. And you would be amazed: at all the bigger technical universities, we find always three hundred to four hundred Indians studying there. We excite them about coming back . . . and they're listening."

Indeed, recent data suggests that the overall brain drain from India has begun to decline, largely owing to the greater economic opportunity and improved standards of life in India in recent years. Only a few decades ago, it was common for more than three-quarters of the IITs' graduating classes to emigrate to the United States; today, that number is estimated to be closer to 10 percent. Although they might be well received and welcomed back by family and friends, Indians returning from abroad are especially heralded by Indian companies. These repats return with not only their talent but also their connections, an improved understanding of developed markets, and world-class business and management experience.

Protecting Intellectual Property

The Indian IP regime has historically denied composition patents for chemicals, foods, and drugs (but supported process patents), as well as all forms of patent protection for agricultural and horticultural products. The context for such restrictive legislation, which was enacted in 1970, highlighted the need to protect national interests, because foreign entities held most of the patents at that time. Widespread fears predicted that foreign patents would prevent domestic competition with imported items, such that Indians could not access goods at cheaper prices. As we noted previously, the original legislation may have helped protect the pharmaceutical industry, but the overall result was a general lack of sophistication when it came to the importance of IP and its protection. Since the mid-1990s, the Indian government therefore has issued forth a series of amendments to the IP regime; a landmark was the harmonization of India's IP regime with the global TRIPS standards in 2005. The numbers since then tell an encouraging story: in 2008, there were 35,218 patent applications filed in India, double the 17,500 filings in 2005. The vast majority of these patents (about 25,000) were filed by foreign applicants (versus about 9,000 by domestic firms).[16]

Yet take the case of Novartis, a company that develops many innovative health-care products for consumers worldwide. In 2006, the Indian patent office refused to grant it a patent for the drug Gleevec, which had been developed in the company's Indian labs, because it considered the drug an incremental improvement over the existing Novartis product Imatinib, rather than a newly patentable innovation. Imatinib had become the standard of care for the treatment of certain malignancies (e.g., one type of leukemia, gastrointestinal tumors), and global revenues ranged in the vicinity of $4 billion annually. Novartis brought suit to force the patent, but its appeals were dismissed in an Indian high court. The outcome prompted Daniel Vasella, CEO of Novartis, to complain: "In principle, you can discover in India, you can do research. There has been some progress on the protection of intellectual property but it's not up to the standard that I would expect to make an investment into discovery-led research."[17]

Only time will tell whether the Indian IP regime will eventually gain the same confidence and attributes as its Western counterparts. In the meantime, companies with IP to protect cannot just wait passively for the regime to improve or watch their secrets being stolen. Instead, R&D captives such as Intel and AstraZeneca must continuously work to protect IP, their core business. But how? In our research, we found that many companies work to protect their IP through what we term an *internal IP regime*, or a set of policies and practices that aims to protect the company from IP leakage, regardless of external legislation. This internal IP regime comprises many elements.

First, many MNCs segment their innovation activity. Activities that, if copied, would cause little harm to the company get located in the low-IP regimes. For instance, the impact of any IP breach at AstraZeneca India is limited, because the lab's discovery work is focused just on diseases that afflict the developing world, rather than extending to blockbuster drugs. These drugs have limited financial potential, such as a treatment for tuberculosis (TB), which remains relatively rare in developed countries but prevalent in the poorest parts of the world—where people cannot afford treatment. When AstraZeneca began development in India, TB afflicted more than fifteen million people and caused about two million deaths annually. Since that time, no new TB drugs have been introduced, because their introduction would demand tens of millions of dollars in investment to discover a drug with no blockbuster commercial potential to recoup that investment. The impact of any potential leak, thus, is much lower than it would be for a conventional blockbuster. Anand Balasundaram, AstraZeneca's managing director, explained:

> Scientists in Boston that we work very closely with are okay sharing proprietary information in this domain [TB] because the downside to them in any case is not large, because there is no anticipation of blockbuster TB medication. This would not be the case in other domains, because there is much higher risk of profit erosion with a breach in IP. As such, there is much less competition from other MNCs. If tomorrow we got into cardiovascular [drugs], whether there would still be the same degree of piggybacking of information and work . . . that is a big question. Would I be unwillingly compromising some sort of confidentiality without knowing how much we could enforce the IP concepts here in India? Perhaps.

Other AstraZeneca labs collaborating with research labs in India expressed a willingness to live with the higher degree of potential IP violation. As Balasundaram noted further, "If the research was in a potentially more lucrative drug, the other R&D labs might not have felt quite so open about sharing information." That is, discovery R&D poses significant, high-impact risks only if competitors care about it and the firms cannot protect it through the IP regime.

Second, training and awareness can make a difference, as Vishakantaiah at Intel India described: "[Internal IP] begins with a strong focus on corporate security awareness and training; it's part of our new employee orientation so it's taught from day one." Intel's course on managing digital security is typically a one- to two-day program, during which the company puts "a lot of emphasis on ideas, invention, incremental innovation, and patents, so we instill a sense of personal, team, and local pride when researchers file for a patent or an invention disclosure. We also fund IP generation contests, where teams compete to file inventions."

Third, companies manage IP by classifying documents according to their level of secrecy. Bedi at Intel explained: "Certain documents and data were available to only a few people and even then only online. This means you can't just print [them], which of course means you can't just walk away with [them]." A story that Bedi recounted clearly emphasized the need for firms to demonstrate a rigorous approach to managing IP, not just talking about it:

On one occasion, an employee reported finding a classified document in the restroom. But instead of saying, "Well, that's okay, let's forgive it," we launched an entire investigation. Each employee was interviewed, and we found that a contract worker had printed it and walked to the restroom with it and simply forgot it there. So the message went back to his contracting employer, saying that this is unacceptable behavior; the message went back to the entire team that this is not acceptable. It's a fact; how seriously you view IP protection is how seriously your employees will view it.

Furthermore, Intel conducts annual risk analyses in which every engineering team reviews potential IP exposure. Finally, when Intel employees leave the firm, they participate in an exit interview—an imperative, considering the high turnover associated with the rapid growth of R&D and related industries in India. Bedi explained how Intel handles the turnover matter: "Of course, a company in start-up mode often will go to any length to get the right people for their core team, which often means paying exponentially more just to get them on board. In our legal exit interview, we are basically being very up-front and clear about the fact that having worked for Intel, [the employees] are subject to a set of specific legal restrictions upon departure. They sign a document so that saying, 'I didn't know I wasn't supposed to take that information with me' isn't an option in the future."

Putting the "Venture" Back into Indian Venture Capital

Even if Indian innovators, particularly entrepreneurs, can overcome weak IP regimes and find talent among the shortages, they still must address the challenge of access to capital. India has a growing and active venture capital industry, but with many global and domestic players jostling for investment opportunities, certain peculiarities of the industry's development conspire to make access to capital difficult, especially for entrepreneurs who aim to design global products.

A brief history might help clarify the situation. The first wave of interest in India's venture capital industry occurred during the dot-com boom. But after the bust in 2001, the few venture capitalists left standing, and a few who followed in their footsteps, exhibited sharply diminished appetites for risk. At the same time, their desire to demonstrate high returns in the Indian markets grew. These preferences, combined with the enormous opportunities for investing in undercapitalized public companies and scaling up profitable private businesses (especially through franchise networks), led companies to avoid risks. The result: a venture capital industry without much sense of "venture." Scaling up a coffee shop chain or a pathology laboratory guarantees returns; investing in an entrepreneurial idea for what could be the next Apple does not necessarily guarantee them—because it might *not* be the next Apple!

Fortunately, though, this situation is slowly changing. Some venture capital funds, such as Sequoia, explicitly have decided to pursue an entrepreneurship cluster, in addition to following growth capital models. Helion targets only ventures that capitalize on traditional strengths in software, turn their service offerings into products or offer products as a service, and are Internet based. These attributes ensure relatively lower risk, quick time to market, and an ability to overcome lead market-access problems. Thus, several venture-backed start-ups in India today are developing software products to enhance office productivity (Zoho), support mobile Internet advertising (InMobi), and enable graphic data visualization (FusionCharts, Infosoft Global).

Other venture capital funds explicitly target technological innovation. The India Innovation Fund is headed by P. V. Rajesh Rai, who recently described the fund's investment strategy:

We are looking to invest in innovation-driven, early-stage, India-focused companies. We feel there is a serious lack of capital in this space. I have been tracking the Indian early-stage market for a few years. Quality and quantity of early-stage deal flow has gone up tremendously. I think the growth has been driven by a host of factors, including global Indians returning to take advantage of the India opportunity, highly driven and educated young Indians who see entrepreneurship as a viable career option, and of course experienced corporate executives who are getting off the corporate ladder to be part of the India growth story through entrepreneurship. Most importantly, with a fast growing and fairly large domestic market and a greater depth of management talent to build quality products, India now offers a reasonable test bed for innovation driven companies.[18]

The India Innovation Fund, funded by NASSCOM and ICICI Knowledge Park Trust, most recently invested in Mitra Biotech, a biotechnology company that focuses on oncology. This start-up was founded by a team of scientists from the Massachusetts Institute of Technology and Harvard Medical School and includes the repat Mallik Sundaram. Notably, Rai is also a repat who returned home to Bengaluru after fourteen years as a venture capitalist in the Washington, D.C., area.

An angel investor community is also becoming more active, filling the gap for funding requests of less than $3 million in the market. For example, the collectively organized Indian Angel Network, founded in 2006, brings together "highly successful entrepreneurs and CEOs from India and around the world who are interested in investing in start-up/early-stage ventures which have the potential of creating disproportionate value."[19] The network invests in a broad spectrum of industries, ranging from agriculture to travel and tourism to IT and life sciences. It agrees to invest up to US$1 million in a firm, then exit over a three- to five-year period through one of several processes, such as an initial public offering, merger and acquisition, or strategic sale. (The network also considers investments of over $1 million, but only through syndication.) Today, angel investors in Indian technology start-ups include some of the best known in Silicon Valley, such as Gururaj Deshpande (founder of Sycamore Networks), Vinod Dham (who helped design Intel's Pentium chip), Vani Kola (founder of RightWorks software), and Vinod Khosla (of Sun Microsystems).

Recommendations

The gaps in India's innovation infrastructure are obvious and have even begun to be discussed explicitly by the country's politicians and leaders. Perhaps, we can take comfort, at least they *are* obvious, whereas just a decade ago, technological innovation was totally removed from the attention of policy makers and firms. In addition, signs of improvement include efforts spearheaded by the private sector. Innovators in India are not waiting for the government to fix the educational system; they are backward-integrating to build talent. Nor are they waiting for the IP regime to achieve perfect protection; rather, they are crafting their own internal IP regimes to overcome the inadequacies of existing legislation. And angel investors and repat venture capitalists refuse to wait for traditional investors, such as Kleiner Perkins Caufield & Byers or Sequoia Capital, to take a funding lead in India. Instead, they are out in front themselves when it comes to Indian innovation. As a result, the situation facing Indian entrepreneurs and innovators has improved, compared with the situation a decade ago. These improvements might not make Bengaluru a second

Silicon Valley—but then again, there is no other "second Silicon Valley" anywhere else in the world, either! However, the innovators and angel investors described in this chapter will improve the prospects that both visible and invisible innovation in India will have global impact. So what does this mean for policy makers and managers?

- MNCs can overcome the weak IP regime by taking the following steps:

  - Actively manage the portfolio of projects across the countries to limit Indian exposure.

  - Raise IP awareness in Indian units.

  - Put in place disciplined processes to prevent (even inadvertent) leakage.

- MNCs (and Indian firms) can help overcome the mirage of mighty labor pools in various ways:

  - Use backward integration into education to produce their own talent.

  - "Adopt" campuses to improve the quality of output.

  - Train the trainer through courses and internships for faculty.

  - Seek repats or bring back qualified Indians who have settled outside India.

- Western policy makers need to retain their advantage over the emerging markets with respect to ease of doing business, transparency, and enforcement of contracts, while continuing to encourage the academic and industry linkages for innovation.

- The innovation regime in India must overcome three key obstacles:

  - Mirage of mighty labor pools

  - Uncertainty around intellectual property protection

  - Venture capital availability

- While the private sector is already attempting to solve some of these issues, ultimately the government has responsibility as well. In particular, Indian policy makers must see increasing educational opportunities and research capacity at all levels as the single biggest constraint to developing India's potential to be an innovation powerhouse.

- Substantial opportunities remain for developing the venture and angel investment sectors in India despite the presence of many global players.

8 The Future of Indian Innovation

The time has come for Indian science to once again think big; think out of the box; and think ahead of the times. This year . . . we also usher in the "Decade of Innovation."

—*Manmohan Singh, Prime Minister of India, 2011 Indian Science Conference Opening Address*

BACK IN THE FIFTEENTH CENTURY, when China was the world's largest economy and its seagoing expertise was substantially ahead of Europe's, the Asian country pioneered new methods of sailing that made it possible for ships to cross oceans more easily. But Europe rather than China was the main beneficiary of these advances, because the geographical fact that Western Europe was only three thousand miles from America's east coast whereas China was eight thousand miles from the west coast of North America meant that the Europeans, instead of the Chinese, colonized the New World and rose to economic dominance. Similarly, it was the United States that invented the Internet, but India has benefited enormously from the subsequent death of distance.

The Internet has made what was considered India's curse and public-policy failure (especially in contrast to the success of China's one-child policy)—the growth of population—into India's biggest competitive asset. Much of the invisible innovation outlined in this book and emerging out of India is possible only because of the Internet. As the developed world and, increasingly, China face an aging population, India's young, dynamic, and growing population provides the world's workforce. It is India's gift to the world, and our message to the world is, embrace it!

Already, the benefits to the developed world in terms of bringing global scale and efficiencies to previously locally optimized processes are apparent. By linking the needs of the rich, developed world to the low-cost labor of India, India has emerged as the world's back office. A new outsourcing industry was born in India and, facilitated by the management innovation of the global delivery model outlined in chapter 5, is rapidly moving into newer, higher-value-added sectors. The spillovers have contributed to increasing standards of living in India and rapid economic growth for the country. About 200 million people have been moved out of poverty in the past two decades, and annual growth rates for the economy are between 8 and 10 percent per annum.

The success of the IT and business process outsourcing sector has attracted many young people into it. An injection of intelligence into this sector has meant that smart and ambitious young people, who may not work in these sectors elsewhere in the world, do so in India. The result, sometimes, is innovation, even in sectors perceived globally as dead end, as we outlined in chapter 4. Furthermore, India's supply of skilled labor has not been able to keep up with this rapid growth. The competition for labor means that compensation levels have risen dramatically, and this has led to the realization that India will lose it low-cost advantage and instead must compete on innovation. In this book, we have demonstrated how innovation is slowly but surely becoming a competitive advantage for India.

To the skeptics' question "Where are the Indian Googles, iPods, and Viagras?" our retort is that it is the wrong question. Much of Indian innovation is invisible. And, given the growth and size of India (as well as China), these are interesting markets in their own right. The visible innovation need not be reverse innovation that must come back to developed markets. For us, the term and mind-set behind reverse innovation smacks of an outdated colonial perspective. The visible innovation emerging from India will be of a different type—one based on frugal engineering (e.g., Nano or GE's ECG machine)—or of the leapfrog variety in new industries (e.g., in mobile technology or alternative energy). Some of this may find a home in the West, but it may matter little even if it does not.

For MNCs from the developed world, we caution that as the markets and the talent pool go east to India and China, it will challenge MNCs' established governance and organizational structures. The sinking skill ladder will force the browning of the top management team. And, if talent, markets, and leadership move East, then it is impossible for the political center of gravity not to follow suit. Questions on whether the MNC's leadership and headquarters should move closer to the East cannot be ignored.

For policy makers in the West, confidence in a Western monopoly on innovation is misplaced. The rise of India will mean that jobs previously considered safe will increasingly become contestable. The resulting downward pressure on wages in some sectors may be inevitable in the short run, though in the long run, India may also become as expensive. Innovation- and technology-leading MNCs such as IBM and GE are ramping up people in India and China while restructuring the workforce in the developed markets. As they are moving their innovation activities to India because of the logic of the market and the talent pool, even the breakthrough innovations like iPod may create more jobs in China (for manufacturing) and India (for software development) than in the United States. Although we do not contest that choices made by policy makers in the West and in India will affect future outcomes, the end of the Western monopoly on innovation seems impossible to reverse.

Two clouds on the Indian horizon, however, can stunt the growth of India as a global innovation hub. First, China could continue its incredible pace of development and effectively steal India's innovation lunch. There is little doubt that China has now some of the best infrastructure for innovation and is investing heavily in building a basic science capability to rival the United States. Unfortunately for China, innovation is often driven by entrepreneurial and rebellious youth. The innovative environment needs an acceptance of chaos and freedom that the Chinese leaders have yet to demonstrate, and the demographics are skewed in India's favor.

Second, the mirage of mighty labor pools in India is beginning to have noticeable effects. The poor infrastructure, slow bureaucracy, and corrupt practices levy additional costs on Indian operations. For the moment, the wage differentials with the developed world are still large enough to make India competitive as an innovation destination. But the demand for Indian skilled labor is growing much faster than the supply. If the government is unable to put in place practices to stimulate education—at both the mass and the specialized levels, in numbers that are several multiples of current graduating classes in each area and at every level, then the favorable labor-cost differential will narrow. There is already some evidence that labor shortages and infrastructure bottlenecks are challenging the cost differentials between India and the developed world. Jeff Immelt, chairman of GE, was quoted in the *Financial Times* as saying the cost difference of running a call center in the United States versus India had narrowed to as little as 10 percent.[1] And India has yet to demonstrate an ability to attract youth from around the world. A 2011 study of top international destinations for students indicated that India attracted only 21,778 students from other countries compared to 690,923 for the United States and 238,184 for China.[2]

The superior physical and educational infrastructure of the developed world and China may make it uneconomical to locate and offshore operations out of India to serve the world. From our perspective, this is the single largest challenge to the development of India's innovation trajectory toward global impact. Unless the country can ramp up its educational infrastructure dramatically to absorb its increasing numbers of young people, it will become a bottleneck not only for Indian innovation, but more generally, for India's economy overall as well as a challenge to the country's social stability. India's large population in such a scenario will become—instead of an asset—a curse and a burden on the country's growth.

Fortunately for policy makers, efforts to fix the educational (and other) infrastructure in India are likely to be not just valuable but also popular with voters today. Recent political contests demonstrate that citizens are beginning to pay attention and consider development, infrastructure, and economic opportunity when they cast their vote, rather than blindly voting their caste, as has too often been the case. Thus, we end the book with a request to India's policy makers—to do what they can to ensure that we will not be proven dead wrong on India's potential as a global innovation hub.

Notes

Chapter 1

1. NASSCOM-McKinsey Report, "Extending India's Leadership of the Global IT and BPO Industries," 2005, www.mckinsey.com/locations/india/mckinseyonindia/pdf/nasscom_mckinsey_report_2005.pdf.

2. Pew Research Center, Pew Global Attitudes Project, "Global Unease with Major World Powers: Rising Environmental Concern in 47-Nation Survey," June 27, 2007, http://pewglobal.org/reports/display.php?ReportID =256.

3. Thomas L. Friedman, *The World Is Flat* (New York: Farrar, Straus, & Giroux, 2005), 264.

4. Ibid., 271.

5. Vikas Bajaj, "With All Its Talent, India Wonders Why Innovation Is Elusive," *New York Times*, December 10, 2009, 17.

6. Historically, *coolie* is a term used to define manual laborers of Asian descent. However, over time, the connotation turned the term into a racial slur or an ethnic nickname for people of Asian descent, especially from India and South Asia.

7. Nirmalya Kumar with Pradipta K. Mohapatra and Suj Chandrasekhar, *India's Global Powerhouses: How They Are Taking on the World* (Boston: Harvard Business School Press, 2009), 209.

8. "The 50 Most Innovative Companies 2010," *Bloomberg/Business-Week*, November 23, 2010, www.businessweek.com/interactive_reports/innovative_companies_2010.html.

9. Please see acknowledgments for details of the people interviewed, and coauthors on research projects.

10. S. S. Kshatriy, *Silicon Valley Greats: Indians Who Made a Difference to Technology and the World* (New Delhi: Vikas Publishing House, 2003).

11. Pratt School of Engineering, Duke University, University of California Berkeley School of Information, "America's New Immigrant Entrepreneurs," January 4, 2007, http://people.ischool.berkeley.edu/~anno/Papers/Americas_new_immigrant_entrepreneurs_I.pdf.

12. Ibid.

13. AnnaLee Saxenian, *Local and Global Networks of Immigrant Professionals in Silicon Valley* (San Francisco: Public Policy Institute of California, May 2002), www.ppic.org/content/pubs/report/R_502ASR.pdf.

14. See http://www.sourcingline.com/resources/it-mncs-maintain-rd-expansion-spree-in-india.

15. Rishikesha T. Krishnan, "From Jugaad to Systematic Innovation: The Challenge for India," Utpreraka Foundation, Bangalore, India, 2009.

16. Clive Cookson, "Patent Proof of Rising Innovation," *Financial Times*, May 20, 2011 special insert Engineering: The Future, 1.

17. Vivek Wadhwa, Guillermina Jasso, Ben Rissing, Gary Gereffi, and Richard Freeman, "Intellectual Property, the Immigrant Backlog, and a Reverse Brain-Drain," August 22, 2007, http://ssrn.com/abstract=1008366.

18. Krishnan, "From Jugaad to Systematic Innovation."

19. Joseph Schumpeter, *The Theory of Economic Development* (Boston: Harvard University Press, 1934).

20. Anand Giridharadas, "Outsourcing Moves to the Front Office," *International Herald Tribune*, April 4, 2007, 10.

21. Nivedan Prakash, "MNC R&D in India," *Express Computer*, May 25, 2009, www.expresscomputeronline.com/20090525/1000thissue07.shtml.

22. Note that between the time we began and the time we completed this book, Pfizer's R&D labs in India have expanded, while the U.K. labs that helped develop Viagra have been shut down. See Andrew Jack, "Supply Running Low," *Financial Times*, February 10, 2010, 9.

23. Gideon Rachman, "The West Re-examines the Rat Race," *Financial Times*, June 1, 2010, 13.

24. M. Adrian Mattocks, letter to the editor, *New York Times*, October 26, 2009, 9.

25. Barack Obama, State of the Union address, January 25, 2011, http://www.whitehouse.gov/the-press-office/2011/01/25/remarks-president-state-union-address.

26. See Intel Oregon plan, February 18, 2011, reported in several Web sites including http://tipnews.info/breaking_news/MjM1Mg==/2011/02/18/us_politics_internet_technology.

Chapter 2

1. According to Wikipedia's definitions, CT (computed tomography) is a medical imaging method that employs tomography created by computer processing, and PET (positron emission tomography) is a nuclear medicine imaging technique that produces a three-dimensional image of functional processes in the body. See http://en.wikipedia.org/wiki/X-ray_ computed_tomography.

2. Tufool Al-Nuaimi, Gerard George, and Phanish Puranam, *Emerging Economies as a Source of Innovation: Patenting by Indian and Chinese R&D Subsidiaries* (2011). Available at http://papers.ssrn.com/sol3/papers.cfm? abstract_id=1854688.

3. Marie Currie Thursby and Jerry Thursby, *Here or There? A Survey on the Factors in Multinational R&D Location* (report to the Government-University-Industry Research Roundtable) (Washington, DC: National Academies Press, September 2006).

4. Vivek Wadhwa, "About the Engineering Gap, . . ." *Bloomberg Businessweek*, December 13, 2005, www.businessweek.com/smallbiz/content/ dec2005/sb20051212_623922.htm.

5. "Allure of R&D Draws Tech Giants to India," *Economic Times*, July 9, 2009.

6. M. Zhao, "Conducting R&D in Countries with Weak Intellectual Property Rights Protection," *Management Science* 52, no. 8 1185–1199.

7. Al-Nuaimi, George, and Puranam, *Emerging Economies as a Source of Innovation*.

8. Suma Athreye and Phanish Puranam, "India and China: Their Role in the Global R&D Economy," working paper (2008). Available at http://www .merit.unu.edu/MEIDE/papers/2008/1202480444_SA.pdf.

9. "i-flex, Infosys Among Top 10 Banking Solution Firms Globally, Finds Survey," *Financial Express*, April 8, 2005, www.financialexpress.com/ news/iflex-infosys-among-top-10-banking-solution-firms-globally-finds-survey/130896/0.

10. "Salary Survey for Country: United States," Pay Scale Web page, May 3, 2011, www.payscale.com/research/US.

11. NASSCOM, "Captives in India: Adding Value to Global Business," executive summary, August 27, 2010, www.nasscom.in/upload/research_ report/captive/Executive_Summary.pdf.

12. Nirmalya Kumar with Pradipta K. Mohapatra and Suj Chandrasekhar, *India's Global Powerhouses: How They Are Taking on the World* (Boston: Harvard Business Press, 2009).

Chapter 3

1. Raja M. Mitra, "India's Emergence as a Global R&D Centre," Working Paper R2007:012, Swedish Institute for Growth Policy Studies, 2007.

2. "Wipro Emerges Leader Among Global R&D Service Providers: Study," *Economic Times,* May 18, 2011, http://articles.economictimes.indiatimes.com/2011-05-18/news/29555878_1_r-d-offshoring-r-d-outsourcing-india-r-d.

3. For the accounts of R&D outsourcing at Wipro and Dr. Reddy's Laboratories, we draw heavily on Saikat Chaudhuri and Phanish Puranam, "R&D Services at Wipro Technologies: Outsourcing Innovation?" Case 50 (Philadelphia: Wharton School Case Series, 2009); and Niraj Gelli and Chakrapani Tummalapalli, under the supervision of Phanish Puranam, "Aurigene Discovery Technologies," Case CS-03–14 (London: Aditya Birla India Centre at London Business School of the Indian School of Business, 2003), respectively.

4. "Aurigene in Drug Discovery Tie-ups," *Business Line,* February 4, 2007, www.thehindubusinessline.com/2007/02/04/stories/2007020400670200.htm.

5. Aurigene Discovery Technologies, "Aurigene and Forest Laboratories to Collaborate on Development of Novel Oral Therapeutics for Obesity and Metabolic Disorders," company Web page, February 2, 2007, www.aurigene.com/wp-content/themes/js-o4w/news_more.php?nid=13.

6. Kirsty Barnes, "India Now Second Only to US as R&D Powerhouse," *in-Pharma,* February 27, 2006, www.in-pharmatechnologist.com/Industry-Drivers/India-now-second-only-to-US-as-R-D-powerhouse; BioSpectrum, "Bio-Active India," *BioSpectrum,* August 2003, http://biospectrumindia.ciol.com/advertising/bs.asp.

7. For a review and model of optimal sourcing strategies, see, for instance, Phanish Puranam, Ranjay Gulati, and Sourav Bhattacharya, "How Much to Make and How Much to Buy? Explaining Optimal Plural Sourcing Strategies," *Strategic Management Journal,* September 27, 2006, available at http://ssrn.com/abstract=932606.

8. This comparison was suggested to us by our colleague Professor Bruce Weber at London Business School.

Chapter 4

1. Prabodh Chander Sharma et al., "Opportunities of Generic Drugs in India," *Internet Journal of Third World Medicine* 8, no. 1 (2009), www.ispub

.com/journal/the_internet_journal_of_third_world_medicine/volume_8_
number_1_17/article/opportunities-for-generic-drugs-in-india.html.

2. The section on Bharat Forge draws from Nirmalya Kumar with Pradipta K. Mohapatra and Suj Chandrashekhar, *India's Global Powerhouses: How They Are Taking on the World* (Boston: Harvard Business School Press, 2009).

3. The section on 24/7 Customer draws from Karin Baye and Phanish Puranam, "24/7 Customer: Reading the Customer's Mind," case study no. 310–203-1 (London Business School, 2010).

4. The section on DenuoSource draws from Amit Ramchandani and Phanish Puranam, "DenuoSource: Turning Art into Science," working paper (London: Aditya Birla India Centre, London Business School, 2010).

Chapter 5

1. Julian M. Birkinshaw, Gary Hamel, and Michael Mol, "Management Innovation," *Academy of Management Review* 33, no. 4 (2008): 825–845.

2. We focus on the management innovation of the global delivery model because this model has global impact and is related to innovation. Of course, there may be many other management innovations in India relating to family business groups, public sector enterprises, nongovernmental organizations, and so on.

3. K. Srikanth and P. Puranam, "Coordination Within vs. Across Firm Boundaries," working paper, London Business School, January 11, 2010, http://ssrn.com/abstract=1534632.

4. K. Srikanth and P. Puranam, "Integrating Distributed Work," *Strategic Management Journal,* in press.

5. Joe Leahy, "Indian Visual Effects Groups Tap US," *Financial Times,* May 31, 2010, 6.

6. For a study indicating that cross-border flows of information, goods, investment, and services are not nearly as globalized as people might imagine, see Pankaj Ghemawat, "Why the World Isn't Flat," *Foreign Policy,* February 14, 2007.

7. This section draws from Srikanth and Puranam, "Integrating Distributed Work."

8. See also Gabriel Szulanski, "Exploring Internal Stickiness: Impediments to the Transfer of Best Practice Within the Firm," *Strategic Management Journal* 17 (1996): 27–43.

9. Srikanth and Puranam, "Integrating Distributed Work."

10. Srikanth and Puranam, "Coordination Within vs. Across Firm Boundaries."

Chapter 6

1. Thomas L. Friedman, *The World Is Flat* (New York: Farrar, Straus, & Giroux, 2005).

2. Nirmalya Kumar with Pradipta K. Mohapatra and Suj Chandrasekhar, *India's Global Powerhouses: How They Are Taking on the World* (Boston: Harvard Business School Press, 2009), 129.

3. Jena McGregor, "The World's Most Innovative Companies," *Business-Week*, April 17, 2008, www.businessweek.com/magazine/content/08_17/b4081061866744.htm.

4. This example and its articulation is inspired by Anand Giridharadas, "Innovation Without Bells and Whistles," *International Herald Tribune*, April 10, 2010, 2.

5. This example draws from Kumar with Mohapatra and Chandrasekhar, *India's Global Powerhouses*.

6. Jeffrey R. Immelt, Vijay Govindarajan, and Chris Trimble, "How GE Is Disrupting Itself," *Harvard Business Review* 87 (October 2009): 56–65.

7. Besides ibid., see also "'Reverse Innovation': GE Makes India a Lab for Global Markets," *India Knowledge@Wharton,* May 20, 2010, http://knowledge.wharton.upenn.edu/india/article.cfm?articleid=4476.

8. Danish Enterprise and Construction Authority, "Philips: SMILE Project," http://www.ebst.dk/publikationer/Corporate_Social_Innovation_-_Case_studies/html/chapter10.htm.

9. Kerry Capell and Nandini Lakshman, "Philips: Philanthropy by Design," *BusinessWeek,* September 11, 2008, www.businessweek.com/magazine/content/08_38/b4100066756397.htm.

10. Ibid.

11. Reena Jain, "Innovation Trickles in a New Direction," *Business-Week,* May 11, 2009, www.businessweek.com/magazine/content/09_12/b4124038287365.htm.

12. Rabin Ghosh, "Ghoshn Back to Praise Frugal Engineering," October 30, 2007, http://www.dnaindia.com/money/report_ghosn-back-to-praising-frugal-engg_1130636.

13. Rishikesha T. Krishnan, *From Jugaad to Systematic Innovation: The Challenge for India* (Bangalore, India: The Utpreraka Foundation, 2010).

14. James Lamont, "The Age of Innovation Dawns," *Financial Times,* June 15, 2010.

15. Jain, "Innovation Trickles in a New Direction."

16. Rina Chandran, "Looking to Profit from Treating India's Poor," *International Herald Tribune,* July 6, 2010, 18.

17. Lamont, "The Age of Innovation Dawns."

18. John Seely Brown and John Hagel III, "Innovation Blowback: Disruptive Management Practices from Asia," *McKinsey Quarterly* (February 2005): 35–45.

19. For Selco, see www.selco-india.com. See also Jim Witkins, "For World's Ills, 'Trickle Up' Solutions," *New York Times,* August 3, 2010, http://green.blogs.nytimes.com/2010/08/03/for-the-worlds-ills-trickle-up-solutions; Amy Yee, "Bringing Light to India's Rural Areas," *New York Times,* September 2, 2010, www.nytimes.com/2010/09/03/business/energy-environment/03iht-rbogsolar.html.

20. Stefan Wagstyl, "Indian R&D Unhindered by Cost Issue," *Financial Times,* January 6, 2011, http://www.ft.com/intl/cms/s/0/02bae652–19b9–11e0-b921–00144feab49a.html#axzz1N4Y0VgYL.

Chapter 7

1. See http://www.doingbusiness.org/rankings.

2. For instance, see Gautam Ahuja, "Inclusive Growth for the Bottom of the Pyramid," Pravasiya Bharatiya Divas Oration, University of Michigan, Ann Arbor, 2011.

3. C. Freeman, "Japan: A New National Innovation System?" in *Technology and Economy Theory,* ed. G. Dosi et al. (London: Pinter, 1988).

4. Adele Hayutin, "Population Age Shifts Will Reshape Global Workforce," Stanford Center on Longevity, Stanford, CA, April 2010, http://longevity.stanford.edu/files/SCL%20Workforce%20Shifts%20Handout%2002-10_FINAL_WEB.pdf.

5. "R&D Talent Drives Product Offshoring to India: Reveals Zinnov Study," *Marketwire,* August 11, 2008, www.marketwire.com/press-release/RD-Talent-Drives-Product-Offshoring-to-India-Reveals-Zinnov-Study-887849.htm.

6. Mark Dutz, ed., *Unleashing India's Innovation: Toward Sustainable Inclusive Growth* (Washington, DC: World Bank Report, 2007).

7. See http://www.znews24.com/faculty-shortage-in-iit-colleges.html.

8. Government of India, National Knowledge Commission, "Engineering Education," www.knowledgecommission.gov.in/downloads/baseline/engineering.pdf.

9. Ashish Singh and Chuck Farkas, "The Indian Opportunity in Pharmaceutical R&D and Manufacturing," Bain Brief (World Economic Forum), Boston, January 2008.

10. Suma Athreye and Phanish Puranam, "India and China: Their Role in the Global R&D Economy," working paper, 2008.

11. Royal Society, "Knowledge, Networks and Nations: Global Scientific Collaboration in the 21st Century," Royal Society, London, March 2011, http://royalsociety.org/uploadedFiles/Royal_Society_Content/Influencing_ Policy/Reports/2011-03-28-Knowledge-networks-nations.pdf.

12. "Nasscom Perspective 2020: Transform Business, Transform India," report, NASSCOM-McKinsey, April 2009, www.mckinsey.com/locations/ india/mckinseyonindia/pdf/NASSCOM_report_exec_summ.pdf.

13. Wikipedia contributors, "Indian Institutes of Technology," *Wikipedia, the Free Encyclopedia,* http://en.wikipedia.org/wiki/Indian_Institutes_of _Technology.

14. Ibid.

15. Amy Kazmin, "Search for a Workable Solution," *Financial Times,* August 30, 2010, 15.

16. "Patent Filing Trend in India," India patent, December 9, 2008, http://indiapatents.blogspot.com/2008/12/patent-filing-trend-in-india .html.

17. Daniel Vasella, interviewed by Reuters, quoted in "Novartis Says Weak IP Protection Makes R&D Impossible," *Seeking Alpha,* November 13, 2009, http://seekingalpha.com/article/173179-novartis-says-weak-ip-protection- makes-india-r-d-impossible.

18. "Nasscom's India Innovation Fund Makes Debut Deal in Mitra Biotech," *VCCircle,* November 23, 2010, www.vccircle.com/500/news/ nasscoms-india-innovation-fund-makes-debut-deal-in-mitra-biotech.

19. Indian Angel Network, "Welcome to IAN: About Us," Indian Angel Web page, 2006, http://www.indianangelnetwork.com/about-us.aspx.

Chapter 8

1. James Lamont, "India Fights Pay Inflation amid Skills Shortage," *Financial Times,* May 13, 2011.

2. See http://www.defence.pk/forums/world-affairs/105390-china-now- global-edu-magnet.html.

Index

About the Authors

Nirmalya Kumar, one of the world's leading thinkers on strategy and marketing, has taught at Harvard Business School, IMD (Switzerland), London Business School, and Northwestern University (Kellogg School of Management).

As an author, Nirmalya has previously written five books, four of which have been published by Harvard Business Press: *Marketing as Strategy* (2004), *Private Label Strategy* (2007), *Value Merchants* (2007), and *India's Global Powerhouses* (2009).

Dr. Kumar is an outlier among marketing professors, having accomplished the rare feat of publishing six articles each in both the *Journal of Marketing Research* (the premier journal for marketing academics) and the *Harvard Business Review* (the premier journal for business practice). These, and other articles, have attracted five thousand and two thousand citations on Google Scholar and Social Science Citation Index, respectively.

As a consultant, coach, and conference speaker, Nirmalya has worked with more than fifty *Fortune* 500 companies in sixty countries. He has served on several boards of directors, including billion-dollar-plus companies and companies included in India's stock indices.

These various accomplishments have led to more than five hundred press appearances, six European case (ECCH) adoption awards, as well as several teaching, research, and lifetime achievement honors. In 2010, Speaking.com voted him among the top five marketing speakers worldwide; the *Economic Times* placed him sixth on the list of Global Indian Thought Leaders; and the *Economist* referred to him as a "rising superstar" in its cover story "The New Masters of Management."

Phanish Puranam is School Chair Professor of Strategy and Entrepreneurship at the London Business School and Chair of the School's PhD Program.

Phanish studies the design and management of collaborative structures within corporations (i.e., between divisions or departments) and between corporations (i.e., alliances and acquisitions). Widely regarded as one of the most published scholars at the cutting edge of research on strategy and organization, Phanish's research on topics such as the structuring of alliance and outsourcing arrangements, postmerger integration, interdivisional collaboration, and reorganizations has appeared in the best internationally reputed academic journals. In addition, he has worked with companies such as Deutsche Bank, Microsoft, 24/7 Customer, Unisys, Tata Consulting Services, IBM, the UK's National Health Service (NHS), and CapGemini in advisory or training roles on these topics. His theoretical work involves mathematical and computational analysis of collaborative structures, and his empirical work focuses on European and U.S. companies with an interest in India, as well as Indian companies that are actively globalizing.

Phanish obtained his PhD at the Wharton School of the University of Pennsylvania and joined the faculty of London

Business School in 2001. When he was promoted in January 2010, he was the youngest among the ranks of full professors at London Business School. In 2011, he was listed among the "World's 40 Best Business School Professors Under the Age of 40" by the Poets & Quants social network. He has held affiliate scholarly appointments with other institutions such as the Advanced Institute of Management (UK), the Mack Center for Emerging Technologies (Wharton), and the Indian School of Business.